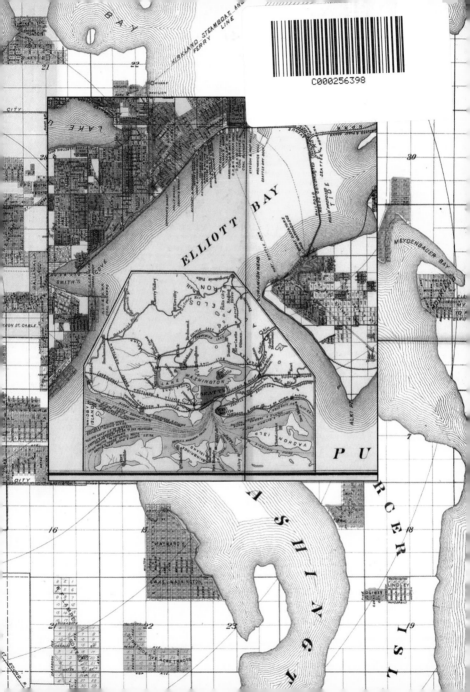

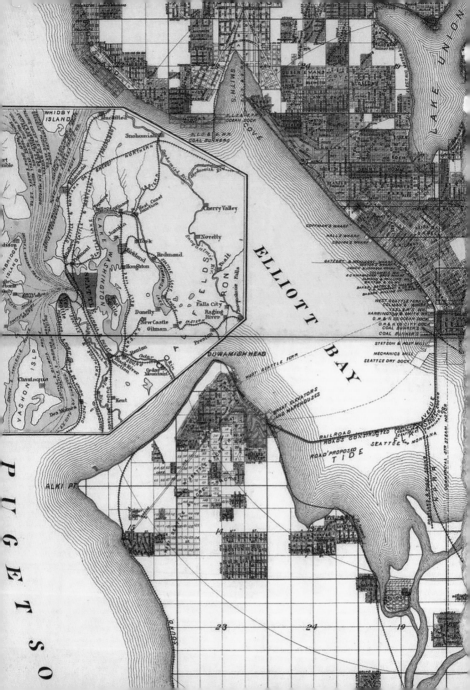

SEATTLE

COCKTAILS

AN ELEGANT COLLECTION
OF OVER 100 RECIPES
INSPIRED BY THE EMERALD CITY

NEIL RATLIFF

CIDER MILL
PRESS

BOOK
PUBLISHERS
KENNEBUNKPORT, MAINE

SEATTLE COCKTAILS

ISBN-13: 978-1-64643-247-9
ISBN-10: 1-64643-247-9

This book may be ordered by mail from the publisher. Please include $5.99 for postage and handling. Please support your local bookseller first!

Books published by Cider Mill Press Book Publishers are available at special discounts for bulk purchases in the United States by corporations, institutions, and other organizations. For more information, please contact the publisher.

Cider Mill Press Book Publishers
"Where good books are ready for press"
PO Box 454
12 Spring Street
Kennebunkport, Maine 04046
Visit us online!
cidermillpress.com

Typography: Haboro Contrast, Avenir, Copperplate, Sackers, Warnock

Photography Credits on page 249

Printed in China

1 2 3 4 5 6 7 8 9 0
First Edition

CONTENTS

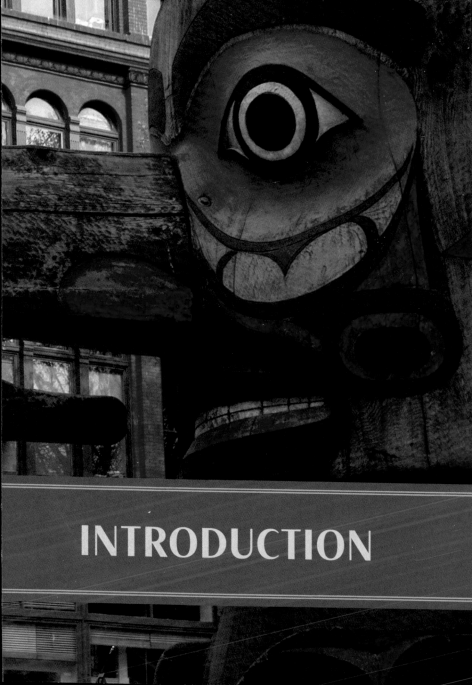

INTRODUCTION

TURN OF LOGS AT
NO 2 ROAD DONKEY
DAVIDSON AN CASKEY
CAMPS

I f the history of Seattle was equal to the height of the Space Needle, then its celebrated cocktail scene would start at the rotating restaurant, about 500 feet up. Seattle has forever been a town of beer and wine, as Washington State grows some of the world's best hops and the Cascadia wine region produces incredible grapes. Locals happily drank Rainier and Olympia beer out of the can, or sipped pinots from the Columbia Valley. Most choices facing bar guests concerned the hoppiness of the beer they wanted, selecting red or white wine with dinner, or deciding whether to go with "up" or on the rocks for their vodka martinis. At least, until future legendary barman Murray Stenson came along. Seattle's original drink-slinger-with-a-smile, he began dusting off old cocktail almanacs from thrift stores and introducing locals and tourists alike to the craft of serving spirits with spirit.

Before white settlers arrived in the 1850s, Puget Sound was inhabited by the Coast Salish peoples, notably the Suquamish and Duwamish. The first village—upon which Pioneer Square sits today—was named Seattle in honor of Chief Sealth of the Duwamish. Soon, the lumber trade boomed and connection to the Transcontinental Railroad triggered explosive growth. Rebuilding efforts after the Great Fire of 1889 were completed just as the city swelled yet again with gold hunters trekking to the Yukon. They came from all over the world: Scandinavia, Africa, Japan. The first half of the twentieth century established Seattle as a flourishing, diverse center of trade and industry, home to the tallest skyscraper in the western United States, the maker of airplanes, and source of the timber that built America. The second half of the twentieth century cemented Seattle's legacy as a hub for technology, the gateway to Asia, a live music capital, a haven for craft distilleries, and the Most Livable City in America. It is during this era that Murray Stenson picked up a shaker and strainer and started the Emerald City's cocktail movement.

MURR THE BLUR

Born in eastern Washington, Murray's family moved to the blue-collar Seattle suburb of Kirkland in the 1960s. He got his first job as a shoe salesman after attending Shoreline Community College. Bouncing around for a while, he found himself tending bar for the first time at Benjamins in Bellevue in the 1970s. He honed his now-famous mechanical technique for working the service well while he developed his "sense of space behind a bar." It was his devotion to technique that allowed his speed to develop, eventually earning him the moniker "Murr the Blur" for his whirlwind efficiency.

One day, after a rough shift, Murray quit Benjamins in solidarity with a coworker. Looking for new employment, he gave her a ride so she could submit a job application at Henry's Off Broadway in downtown Seattle. While he waited for her, Henry's owner recognized Murray and offered him a job on the spot working behind the main bar. The self-described introvert immediately found himself forced to converse with guests. "I had to talk to them!" he explains. "It took me six months to shake off the nerves. Eventually, I figured it out." Though he may have started his bartending career sheepishly, the persona that Murray began to cultivate at Henry's would go on to become the

inspiration for many of his apprentices who opened their own bars years later.

Moving on to jobs at the iconic Oliver's, Daniel's Broiler, and Ray's Boathouse, Murray "worked a lot" in the 1980s. He refined his tradecraft, recalling obscure recipes from old cocktail books he would find at thrift shops. He practiced the art of conversation, committed his movements to muscle memory, and perfected the skills of a master bartender. In 1990, he began working at Il Bistro, the bar at which he would spend the next decade and shape into a rite of passage for up-and-coming bartenders, who sat attentively and filled their notebooks with Murray's teachings. This "First Class" of pupils credit Murray with instilling in them a passion for excellent customer service and fascination with mixology. Murray's first and most influential disciple, Ben Dougherty, would soon open his own cocktail bar and influence a new generation of bartenders.

ZIG ZAG CAFE AND THE COCKTAIL RENAISSANCE

Ben Doughtery had been working in New York City's restaurant scene, marveling at the style and glamour of the trendy haunts, while noting the absence of what he considered true hospitality. He returned to Seattle in 1991 and

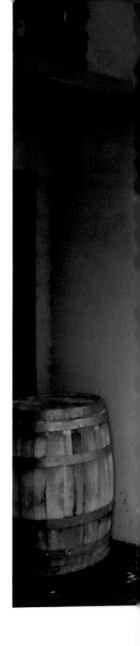

soon discovered Murray, working at Il Bistro. "I studied everything he did," recounts Ben. "I decided then that I wanted to be a bartender, I wanted to bartend like Murray. He inspired me." Ben landed a job at Macchiavelli, and on nights off he would perch on a stool at Il Bistro and pick Murray's brain, absorbing his aura and style. In 1999, he partnered with Kacy Fitch to open Zig Zag Cafe behind the iconic Pike Place Market.

"We decided to build a bar that would allow us to make anything," explains Ben. "I wanted to take the style I witnessed in New York and combine it with the service of my mentor, Murray Stenson." A bar built by bartenders, for bartenders—no televisions, no sidewalk A-frame chalkboards with whiskey puns begging passersby to come inside, and definitely no hollow service.

Within six months of Zig Zag's opening, Murray would leave his job of ten years at Il Bistro to tend bar with Ben and Kacy, which is perhaps what the pair had in mind all along. One day, Murray stepped into another local bar in Pioneer Square and discovered that their cocktail program was nearly identical to Zig Zag's. "The bartender was a nice guy," Murray remembers, "but let's say that he 'borrowed heavily' from us." So the Blur combed through Zig Zag's spirit selection, which had fast become the most eclectic in the city, to come up with a unique cocktail program that could not be easily copied. Knowing that they likely had the only Maraschino liqueur in town, Murray seized upon a recipe from one of his thrift shop books: The Last Word from *Bottoms Up* by Ted Saucier. Little did the Zig Zag team know how significant this would become in the great cocktail renaissance only a few years later.

Seattle experienced a cocktail resurgence around 2005, and within a few years the city bars had transformed from old fashioned to Old Fashioned, with Zig Zag playing an integral role. "We influenced the entire cocktails scene," says Ben. Sazeracs, Manhattans, Sidecars, and the ubiquitous Old Fashioned had replaced the usual Martinis and Cuba Libres. As he himself had done with his mentor Murray on so many nights at Il Bistro, soon Ben and his crew were inspiring the latest crop of young and eager bartenders who posted up on Zig Zag's barstools, notebooks in hand and questions aplenty. Two of those cocktail scholars would go on to influence the scene in their own distinct way: Keith Waldbauer and Casey Robison.

KEITH WALDBAUER, CASEY ROBISON, AND THE WASHINGTON BARTENDERS GUILD

After stints in Illinois, Michigan, Vermont, and Colorado, Keith Waldbauer moved back to Seattle in 2005, at the genesis of the cocktail renaissance. He started working shifts at Union, the first restaurant in Ethan Stowell's Seattle portfolio. When Keith arrived, "there was no bar culture to speak of. Zig Zag was the main game in town," he recalls. In no time, he was at Murray's bar, drinking it all in. "I had already been bartending for a long time, but I normally worked in restaurants. I did not know much about cocktail history or classic cocktails," says Keith. "Once I got introduced to obscure classics at Zig Zag by Ben, Murray, and Kacy, I was hooked." After they would finish up their own shifts around town, new apprentices would gather for their nightly lessons. "We all kind of wound up at Zig Zag," says Keith. "On a Sunday night, I remember looking across the bar and seeing four or five people with notebooks. They were all bartenders taking notes from Murray." One of those learned observers was up-and-coming bartender Casey Robison.

Casey started off as a barback in 2003 at local Irish pub The Clever Dunce. "I had gotten into the action of bartending," he recalls. "I had

started getting curious about different spirits. But this is 2003—there was nothing! We were the top seller of cherry-flavored vodka. We had a house drink called the Cherry Bomb, mixed with cranberry juice and energy drinks," he says with a laugh. A colleague suggested that he stop by Zig Zag one night after work. "My friend told me, 'If you are into cocktails, go see Murray.'"

"So Andrew Dolan [of Liberty Bar] and I went down. We were punk kids," Casey explains with a smile. "I told Murray 'I hear you're a great bartender; make me something!' He likely hated me." Murray returned a moment later with a Corpse Reviver #2 and set it in front of Casey. "That was . . . wow. That was new," he says as he raises his arm and proudly shows me a tattoo of that very cocktail. "It was the first drink Murray made me."

Right away, Casey began using his new knowledge to revamp the bar offerings at a local Italian joint, Chez Gaudy. It was 2005, and the cocktail renaissance was at hand. Bartenders were rediscovering forgotten drink recipes, just as Murray Stenson had done in the 1970s and 1980s. A newfound fascination with cocktail culture generated a surge in bar creativity around the country. Out were Strawberry Daiquiris and Appletinis; in were Boulevardiers and Negronis. "*Vintage Cocktails and Forgotten Spirits* by Ted Haigh had just come out, and that's what everyone was reading," remembers Casey. "I basically took everything from that book and put it on the menu." He left that bar to work at Can Can, where he met Keith. The two bonded, and were soon discussing the need to solidify their small, but growing, community of knowledge-hungry Seattle bartenders.

"There were ten people doing cool things," recalls Keith about the mid-2000s. "We were all separated, but aware of what the others were doing. There was no community at that time. We all eventually met and liked each other." One time, after Keith learned that he had missed a local symposium about cocktail bitters, he lamented to his new colleague Casey that they needed to form a group with a mission to cultivate and share bar industry craft. That was the genesis of the Washington State Bartenders Guild.

Formed by sixteen like-minded drink slingers in 2008, the WSBG "took a year or two to gel," remembers Keith. "Once it did, we were, well, not inseparable but. . ."

"Pretty close!" interjects Casey.

"Yeah, you're right. The community became pretty tight pretty fast, and it's been like that ever since," says Keith with a smile.

"The Guild did not start at Zig Zag," clarifies Casey. "That's where we went to *learn* about cocktails." They experimented, refined recipes, and shared ideas at 611 Supreme Bar in the Capitol Hill neighborhood, which became the bartenders' bar. After filling notepads from the brains of Murray and Ben, this generation of bartenders would congregate on their nights off "to throw down." This was how the new alliance of Seattle's serious bartenders came to be—playing around, talking shop, and venturing into new creations. "That was an important part of my upbringing," Casey reminisces. Soon, guild members were running their own cocktail-forward watering holes around the city, like Barrio, Vessel, Tavern Law, Liberty, and Canon.

HOW IT'S GOING

"Fast forward to today," says Keith, when asked about the current state of the Seattle cocktail scene. "We are introducing people to rye, to Old Fashioneds, the classic drinks that are not Martinis. Seattle didn't know what a Sazerac was. "Now [at the Doctor's Office, the bar he operates with Casey], we have people coming in asking for egg white drinks," Keith says with delight. "The other day, I had someone come in and ask for a Bee's Knees. I'm thinking, 'Where did you come from?' I love it!"

As testament to how influential Murray's "First Class" was, Seattle evolved from a beer and wine town into a global cocktail destination

caption TK?

within a decade of Murray stepping behind the bar at Zig Zag, all because one affable barman had demonstrated to the industry how to elevate its game and practice tradecraft. "When I got started," recalls Keith, "we were all mixing with sour mix. Now, *everything* is fresh." The progression extended beyond mixers, however. While working at Barrio, Casey ran Half-Price Mezcal Monday promotions. Many of the barstools were occupied by curious bartenders from all around.

"I'm half joking, but Seattle is now a mezcal town, and I'm responsible for that," he says.

"Our guests ask for mezcal cocktails five or six times per night!" exclaims Keith. "That *never* happened before."

With the cocktail renaissance came not only these new cocktail crafters, but a new type of customer too. When asked what the biggest change has been in the local scene since the explosion of 2005, Keith has a quick answer. "The sophistication of the drinkers is the most revelatory thing. It's amazing to me, the level of knowledge that the people have. That's a credit to Seattle bartenders."

MUST-KNOW SEATTLE PHRASES

• **THE MOUNTAIN'S OUT:** This means that the skies are clear and sunny, and the vista is filled with the mighty Mount Rainier. The University of Washington owns all the airspace between its campus and the mountain, so the view of Rainier from Suzzallo Library is never obstructed.

• **BEAST MODE:** To go absolutely berzerk at your task; this was the nickname of legendary NFL running back Marshawn Lynch, Seattle's most beloved player, thanks to his infamous touchdown run against the New Orleans Saints in 2010.

• **12TH MAN**: Refers to the crowd at Lumen Field during Seahawks football games; each team fields eleven players, with the 12th man as the rowdy pack of rabid, screaming fans.

• **RIDE THE SLUT:** The South Lake Union Trolley (S.L.U.T.) traverses downtown Seattle; the city has embraced the saucy acronym, with Ride the SLUT T-shirts available in Pike Place Market's tourist shops.

• **MEET AT THE PIG:** To use the iconic brass pig at the entrance to Pike Place Market as a meeting spot; from here you can watch the fishmongers throw the fish for enthralled tourists before sampling the delights of Seattle's seafood cathedral.

• **ORDERING A "RAHN-YAY" OR "OLY":** To order a Rainier (as if it were French and fancy—which it is not) or Olympia beer.

SEATTLE BARTENDING

Everything in Washington State is highly regulated, and serving booze is no exception. All those who prepare and serve alcohol must be 21 years of age and carry a Class-12 permit, obtained after completing a four-hour class and passing the subsequent quiz. Bartenders must be learned not only in the fundamentals of serving alcohol, but in the numerous and consequential state laws as well. The rules that govern imbibing are strict, going so far as to require the bartender to remove the drink from any intoxicated guest ("I once got in a fistfight doing that," recalls Murray). Another law prevents the selling of alcohol for less than its purchase price—no free shots or two-for-ones in the Emerald City!

While perhaps not enshrined in law, there are other unspoken requirements of Seattle bartenders—none more important than local product knowledge. Seattleites are rightfully proud of their beer, wine, and spirits. Bar patrons who are visiting the city should be guided toward a local IPA, pinot noir, or small-batch bourbon made in the area. To visit the Pacific Northwest and drink imported beer or spirits is to not visit at all. It's a special delight to serve someone their first Manny's Pale Ale or Mac and Jack's African Amber and watch their new hoppy enlightenment take hold in real time. If you have seen it advertised during the Super Bowl, don't order it while in Seattle. Any bartender worth their salt will have several incredible and unique beers for you to try, and the same goes for gin, whiskey, and tequila—we make it all here.

The second unspoken requirement of Seattle bartending is the skill of conversation. When I first moved to Seattle from Central Florida, my friends back home and my new friends in the city would ask me what the biggest cultural difference between the two places was. My answer was always the same: conversation means something more substantial out here. Living in or visiting the Pacific Northwest, you will notice that getting your latte at the coffee shop or your Rainier Beer at the pub will take an extra minute or two compared to other places in the United States. It's not because people move more slowly out here (okay, not *only* because of that), but rather because chitchat is elevated, more substantive. An innocuous "How is your day going?" from the barista will often solicit a heartfelt, thoughtful, and earnest response from the customer, quickly engaging the two in talk of politics, philosophy, or music while the barista froths the milk. Instead of the usual fluff chat—no one cares what the weather report says—try commenting to the bartender that you like the song playing over the speaker, or their weird tattoo, or the rainbow-colored crosswalks on the streets. You will find yourself immediately engaged in a pleasant conversation and will almost certainly learn something interesting. It also goes without saying that all bartenders should stay informed about the hometown teams—the Seahawks (American football), Sounders (soccer), Kraken (ice hockey) and Mariners (baseball). Do not, however, mention the Seattle Supersonics. Ever.

HAPPY HOUR

Seattle is more obsessed with happy hour than any other city in America. Locals quickly sniff out the best afternoon deals on draft beers, raw oysters, and craft cocktails, and weekdays from 3 to 6 p.m. are almost as important as Friday and Saturday nights are to business. When I was bartending at Blueacre Seafood on Olive Avenue, our sixty-seat lounge would buzz like a hive every afternoon as employees from Nordstrom and Amazon rushed from their cubicles upstairs down to the bar for $1 oysters and $3 drafts. Tumbleweeds may roll past the Seattle bars that do not take happy hours seriously, while the bar across the street with cheap sliders and a daily drink special might be standing room only at 4:00 p.m.

There are explanations for Seattle's obsession with happy hour. First, rush-hour traffic in Puget Sound is brutal, and most commuters find it more pleasant (and productive) to spend that time of day watching a few innings of the Mariners game with a dozen Hood Canal oysters, or networking with colleagues over a cold Space Dust IPA, rather than be stuck bumper-to-bumper on Interstate 5. Secondly, many of those who work in the city are in the tech sector, where they enjoy more freedom in their choice of work hours versus the rigid 9-to-5. It is not uncommon for these workers to begin and end their workday much earlier in concert with the East Coast time zone, or begin their day much later, hit happy hour for a quick respite or brainstorming session, then head back to the office until the late evening. Add these factors up, and happy hour is to Seattle what the siesta is to Barcelona.

SUNSHINE, BRUNCH, AND GAMEDAYS

In the Pearl Jam song "Present Tense," Eddie Vedder ponders: "Do you see the way that tree bends?/ Does it inspire?/ Leaning out to catch the sun's rays/ A lesson to be applied." Like a prayer plant, raising and lowering its leaves along with the rising and setting of the sun, successful bars in Seattle are able to take advantage of good weather. The city receives about 160 sunny days per year, the majority of which are only partly so, with sunbreaks in the afternoon sandwiched between overcast mornings and evenings. When the sun shines bright and scares all the clouds from the blue horizon, it is a special thing—summers in the Pacific Northwest are America's best-kept secret. People

spill outside like ants from a disturbed anthill, filling bars for weekday happy hours and packing patios on the weekend from open to close. All of this puts a premium on a bar's ability to adapt to daily changes in volume as it relates to the weather.

Watering holes with lots of outdoor seating are uniquely positioned to profit from these sunny days, as are those with attractive brunch programs. During the summer months, the early sunrises are perfect for a late breakfast ("kegs and eggs") after walking the dog or going for a hike, and many bars open early and offer special menus for the hungry locals and summer tourists alike. A good Bloody Mary is essential for any successful bar, as are Beermosas (light beer with fresh orange juice), Irish Coffees, cold drafts, and sparkling cocktails like French 75s, mimosas, and spritzes. For eats, popular brunch fare includes crab Benedict, crab cakes, fish and chips, clam chowder, and seafood stews.

The schedules of Seattle's sports teams have a huge influence on the legion of sports bars and pubs around the city. Many run special programs during broadcasts of Seahawks, Sounders, Mariners, and Kraken games. A bright Sunday morning in September before a home game at Lumen Field can be the special mix that floods the city's streets with thirsty fans. The Seahawks and Sounders have each won championships in recent years, and Seattle bars welcome a clientele of energetic fans who like to drink and eat before, during, and after their games. All of this means that Seattle bartenders can expect a very different work schedule during the summer than during the dreary winter months.

PULL TABS

Many Seattle bars offer pull tabs, a cousin of the scratch-off lottery ticket wherein patrons purchase small paper "tabs" from the bar and pull the perforated cover from the back sheet to reveal if they have won cash prizes or merchandise. Winning tabs are redeemed at the point of sale, meaning bars that offer them must be able to pay out large sums of money (up to $5,000) to winners when they are redeemed (bars can pay by cash or check). This presents a unique concern to those who work at bars that offer pull tabs; bartenders must be capable of explaining the game, providing tabs (normally kept in multiple large buckets behind the bar, separated by the price of the ticket), and honoring winnings. It is not common for patrons to tip for this service, so while it supplements the bar's revenue, it does not normally benefit the bartender; etiquette dictates that bar patrons ask for pull tabs when the bartender has the time to service them. Asking for tickets while the bartender is flying around during a rush constitutes a faux pas—and in this case patrons should supplement their tips to reflect the extra work for the bartender.

THE LEGEND:

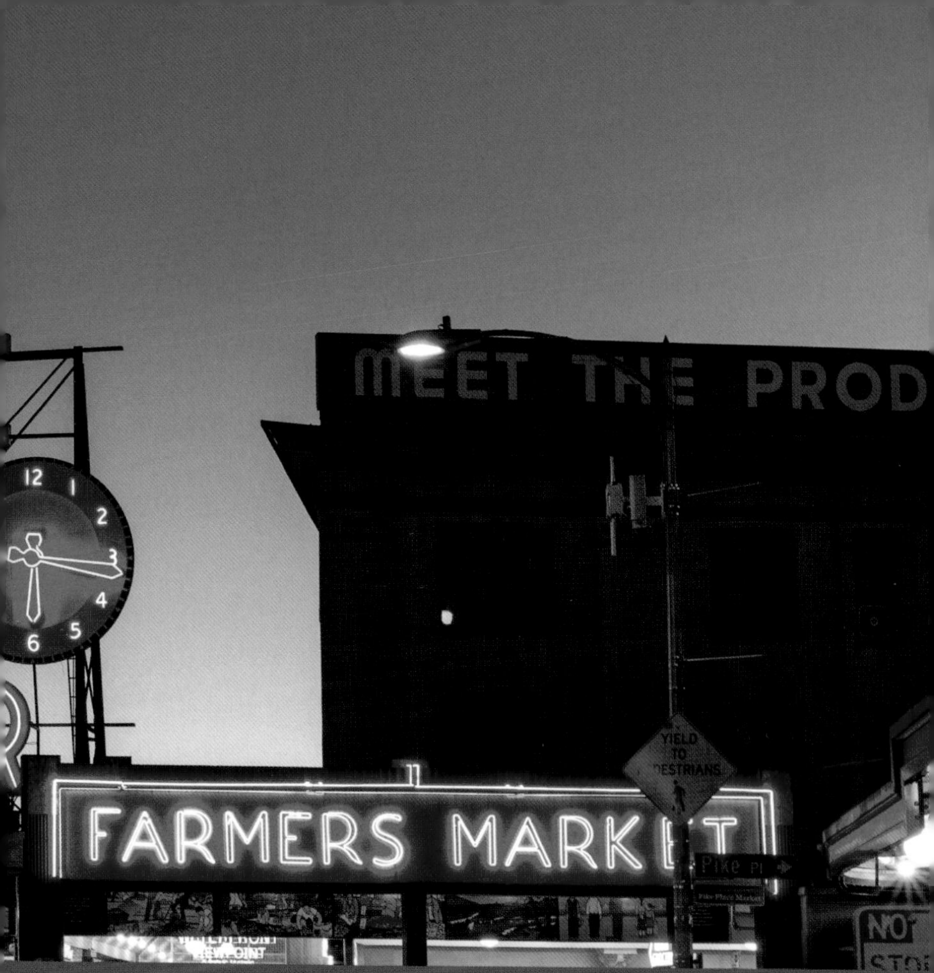

MURRAY STENSON

E very successful bar owner in Seattle credits Murray Stenson as the Godfather of the local cocktail scene, and many of them credit Murray as their personal inspiration as well. All consider it a privilege to sit at his bar. He combines encyclopedic knowledge with a jovial approach and a focus on service to form the perfect bar persona.

I texted Murray about meeting for an interview. I suggested that we have coffee at KEXP, the coffee shop inside Seattle's legendary listener-powered radio station. "Perfect!" he replied. "I will be in a black windbreaker. Often mistaken for George Clooney." I let him know that I have bright dyed-blue hair and I would be easy to identify. "Neil," he wrote, "I hate guys bragging about having hair." I liked him instantly.

Murray is the most important character in Seattle's cocktail story. He is also the most revered, credited, and lionized living person I have ever met. The bartenders he taught and inspired are fiercely defensive of his legend and his privacy; it took me weeks of chatting with his colleagues to earn their trust, and even longer to get Murray's phone number. "He is retired and very private," one bar owner told me. "I'm not going to introduce you. What do you want to know about him?"

After I was finally enjoying a latte with him, I understood. Murray is remarkably jovial, ingratiating, and funny. I asked him about winning the Bartender of the Year award in 2010 from the Tales of the Cocktail Foundation in New Orleans. "They sent me an award plate," he deadpans. "I use it for my cold cuts. People would come up to me and say 'You're the Best Bartender of the Year!', and I would say 'No, I'm the *Best-Looking* Bartender of the Year.'"

THE STORY BEGINS

"I was never one of the cool kids in school," Murray says. The iconic barman learned the craft of hospitality and the art of conversation, you see—they were not natural gifts. "I was afforded the potential to learn about drinking very gradually. At that time, the accent was on taking care of the customer. Hospitality was the number-one thing, making the customer happy." He wonders aloud if that is still the case.

Starting his career behind the service well at Benjamins, Murray trained himself in the essentials of bartending—proper pouring and shaking, efficiency of movement, and the fluidity of presentation. When he was thrown in front of guests for the first time at Henry's, he practiced his showmanship and dialogue until the shy caterpillar transformed into the bright butterfly he is today. He hit his stride and discovered his aptitude for the craft. "The reason I got into bartending," he explains, "is so I could hang out with all the cool adults, smoking and drinking. I could hang out with those people and get paid for it." He was hooked, and the sky was the limit.

"After a couple of years, I told one of my regular bar guests I'm going to stick with this and asked, 'Who are the best bartenders in town?'" The regular named some of his favorite barkeeps around the city. "I would post up at their bars and learn the basics. I was fortunate, at that time in America, drinking was at a nadir. Everyone was doing drugs instead."

It was a very different time, indeed. When he started work at the Carousel Room at Oliver's in 1978, it was the first cocktail bar in the entire state with windows—decency at the time required drinkers to go about their business away from public view. The city also enforced morality by forbidding the sale of packaged alcoholic beverages on Sundays. "In those days," Murray explains, "if you were a woman and unescorted, you could not sit at the bar by yourself. It was really primeval." (His time at Oliver's was not absent of fun, however; one evening he had to cut off an intoxicated guest, and when Murray removed the man's drink it came to fisticuffs).

Ben Dougherty: "He is extremely intelligent. He has an uncanny memory. He did it better than anyone else: The Master. Murray has the ability to connect with you and make you feel special"

Murray worked stints of differing lengths at bars around Seattle through the 1980s, following the money. When he wasn't being quizzed by his bartender disciples, he was getting job offers from restaurant owners who wanted to steal Murray and his legion of followers. Wherever he went, success seemed to follow. "One of the highlights of my forty-plus years of bartending was one night working with Jim Luby," the man Murray credits as the best bartender he ever worked with. "We had a full bar, and two deuces [two groups of two people] walked in, and the manager told these people that he could seat them in the dining room for drinks, while they waited for dinner at the bar." Murray erupts with laughter. "That was the best job I ever had."

I was interested to know from where he farmed his collection of old cocktail books, before the era of online procurement. He would scour secondhand stores like Goodwill and occasionally strike gold. "In the early days," he says, "no one was into that stuff. I started collecting books in the early 1980s, I'm a packrat. Back in the 1990s, I would hand out [David] Embury's cocktail books to young bartenders."

"If any of them are reading this, I would like those books back," he quips.

ZIG ZAG, THE COCKTAIL RENAISSANCE, AND TODAY

Murray and I agree that the essence of Zig Zag Cafe, what makes it special, is the ambience. The inviting atmosphere is what draws people in and makes them want to stay. "It amazes me how cozy and warm it is," he says. After spending all of the 1990s inspiring a new generation of bartenders at Il Bistro, Ben Dougherty was finally able to poach Murray away to Zig Zag in 2001, the bar at which he would spend the next decade of his storied career. "The community was close knit—exclusive membership, up until the 2000s," he remembers. "Then it exploded."

As a cocktail celebrity of sorts, Murray's employment is the ultimate endorsement of a Seattle bar, and Zig Zag was soon packed with his loyal regulars. Their revived cocktail caught fire up and down the coasts in bars, books, and magazines, and it was off to the races. When the national cocktail renaissance blossomed in 2005, Zig Zag was positioned as the epicenter of it all; soon, lines would gather at the entrance before they opened. It was like the Beatles playing Ed Sullivan, but for cocktail nerds. "I had a lot of customers from those early days say that they miss that era," Murray says. It seems like a good place, toward the end of our chat, to ask his thoughts on the current cocktail scene, the latest generation of bartenders, and how the industry differs today from his start in the 1970s.

"The hospitality has suffered," he laments. I think a lot of that has gone away, it's something that I have been saying for twenty years. The professionalism of bartenders has increased—their recipes and their methodology. That has been spectacular to a fault." He pauses to choose his next words. "There is . . . a lot of cocktail snobbery that I really hate." Over this, we bonded, as I bemoaned the inaccessibility and manufactured mystique in today's bar scene, that it seems to receive more attention than the tradecraft of accommodation and customer service.

"It grieves me," Murray continues, "that this new generation of bartenders has no experience with hospitality. I had a longtime regular bar guest—since 1990—who went to a bar here in town that had a real hotshot national reputation. He sits at this guy's bar, where the previous customer had spilled water on the countertop." The bartender took his order, served his drink, and never once cleaned the bar. "You have to consider how people are feeling," he says with the certainty of a professor. "You have to read the moment. Hospitality is everything. Focus on what the customer is looking for, what the customer is feeling."

Demitri Pallis: "I had this Christmas tradition: I would start out on December 24 and I'd go buy a stack of freaky Japanese comics to use as my wrapping paper. Then I'd walk up and down Broadway Avenue, I'd buy chocolates and things, I'd buy things at Pike Place Market. I would end up at Il Bistro, and I would watch Murray. You watch the guy, you would think he is blasted on biker crank or something. The guy was so fast. He was just flying around that place. His stories, his product knowledge … I'd just sit there and have my cognac and espresso and I would take in the excitement. I would watch Murray go to town."

THE FIRST CLASS

THE LAST WORD

O.H. BYRON'S MANHATTAN COCKTAIL #2

THE DOCTOR'S OFFICE SPANISH COFFEE

EL NACIONAL

LOVE IN THE TIME OF COVID

BLOODY SCANDI

CRIMSON GARDEN

DOUGLAS FIR SPARKLE

BERRIES & BUBBLES

LIQUID KITCHEN OLD FASHIONED

HONEY MINT CARROT COLLINS

KATHY'S SPICED MANHATTAN

HOLIDAY CRUSH

THE SMOKEY GREEN GODDESS

BUZZED BUTTERED RUM

As Murray Stenson put Seattle on the map for its nascent cocktail bonafides, Ben Dougherty and Kathy Casey were honing their respective crafts, as they forged their own paths through the emerging hospitality landscape. Keith Waldbauer and Casey Robison were inspired to design their own programs and unify the bartender collective in the Washington State Bartenders Guild.

ZIG ZAG CAFE

BEN DOUGHERTY

"We didn't start it—we influenced it. Heavily," says Ben Dougherty.

Ben has a wonderful way with words, effortlessly floating one-liners that would sound absurd coming from someone less confident. He has a calmness about him that makes you wonder if he is a jiujitsu black belt. I don't ask. "Before the cocktail scene, we would just follow our favorite bartenders around and wish they made better drinks."

Tucked away behind Pike Place Market, Ben started Zig Zag with Kacy Fitch and a few other business partners in late 1999. That arrangement quickly evolved into the pair owning it outright. They designed it top-to-bottom as "a place that would allow us to make anything." The first thing that strikes you as you enter Zig Zag is the lighting. It's a perfect mix of soft autumnal copper and candlelight, with the inviting warmth of an Irish pub. The ambience is calming, invoking guests to relax and lower their voices for a cocktail conversation, without even knowing it. There are those with perfect pitch, those with gifted palates and noses, but Zig Zag has mastered Perfect Hue.

The Last Word is an "equal parts" drink, one of those magical recipes that unites ingredients in equivalent proportions to create a sum much greater than its parts. Gin, maraschino, fresh lime juice, and green chartreuse come together in a dance of sweet and sour, an altogether new flavor that sings to the tongue. The team at Zig Zag fell in love with Ted Saucier's inventive cocktail, and started serving it to their regulars and other bartenders—especially those visiting from other parts of the country. In no time, the Last Word was in New York and San Francisco; Zig Zag quickly became the largest purchaser of chartreuse in the United States. The cocktail has become inextricably linked with Murray, Ben, Zig Zag, and Seattle writ large, and was the taproot for the budding cocktail scene.

· THE LAST WORD ·

The fine balance of flavors here guarantees that once you make this drink, it won't be the last time.

◆

GLASSWARE: Nick and Nora

GARNISH: Italian cherry

- ¾ oz. green Chartreuse
- ¾ oz. maraschino liqueur
- ¾ oz. gin
- ¾ oz. fresh lime juice

1. Combine all of the ingredients in a cocktail shaker with ice, shake well, and strain into the glass.

2. Garnish with an Italian cherry on a garnish pick.

THE DOCTOR'S OFFICE

KEITH WALDBAUER AND CASEY ROBISON

Keith Waldbauer is a Seattle-based bartender and consultant with over thirty years of experience in the bar and restaurant industry. He is a former co-owner of Liberty and currently co-runs the bar at The Doctor's Office in the Capitol Hill neighborhood. Globally recognized for his bar training, his cocktails have been published on menus and in books internationally. As a consultant Keith has developed drink programs for numerous bars and restaurants, and he has trained thousands of young bartenders in their craft at hotels throughout the world. He is co-founder of the Washington State Bartenders Guild and has long been a consistent champion of the Seattle hospitality community.

Here are thoughts on Seattle's cocktail scene from Keith Waldbauer (The Doctor's Office in Capitol Hill), in his own words:

"My fascination with cocktails began like a lot of other Seattle people: through the Zig Zag cafe in the early-mid 2000s. I'd already been bartending for a long time, but I normally worked in highly-regarded restaurants. I didn't know much about cocktail history or classic cocktails. Once I got introduced to obscure classics at Zig Zag by Ben, Murray, and Kacy, I was hooked. I started a blog, found the ten or so other people in Seattle who were into these cocktails (that list is amazing to look at now: Paul Clarke, Robert Hess, Anu Apte, Jim Romdall, Rocky Yeh, Casey Robison, Jamie Boudreau, Jay Kuehner, and a few others) and began actively trying to build a community.

"The Guild is still around, educating bartenders and hosting gatherings. And the community has grown very strong in those thirteen years since it was founded. Virtually all out-of-town bartenders who visit Seattle remark on how tight-knit the community is here.

"Seattle has grown up with us. Customers regularly ask for vintage cocktails, and now a community exists where a classic, stirred-only, spirit-forward cocktail bar like The Doctor's Office can do extremely well. We like our Old Fashioneds and Manhattans in Seattle, more so than any other cocktails, and more so than in most cities. I like to think that the Seattle bartender community had something to do with that."

• O.H. BYRON'S MANHATTAN COCKTAIL #2 •

"Turns out the first published recipes for the Manhattan do not look like the Manhattans we make today. O.H. Byron published two recipes: one with dry vermouth, of all things, and another with the sweet vermouth we know today, but it also included dry curaçao. So, I took this recipe and added a touch of saline and a couple dashes of sherry to make this interpretation of the true, original Manhattan."
—Keith Waldbauer

❖

GLASSWARE: Cocktail glass
GARNISH: Cherry on a pick

- 2 oz. bourbon
- ¾ oz. sweet vermouth
- ¼ oz. dry curaçao
- 2 dashes Angostura Bitters
- 2 dashes Pedro Ximénez Sherry
- 2 drops saline solution (200 grams water to 50 grams high-quality salt)

1. Combine all ingredients in a mixing glass with ice, stir well, and strain into a cocktail glass.

2. Garnish with cherry on a pick.

• THE DOCTOR'S OFFICE SPANISH COFFEE •

"No offense to Huber's and their iconic Spanish Coffee, but we wanted to do a Spanish Coffee with more complexity and with actual Spanish ingredients." —Keith Waldbauer and Casey Robison

---

GLASSWARE: Heat-resistant glass

- **Demerara sugar, for rimming**
- **En Fuego Potion**
- **Spanish Coffee Mix**
- **Salted-Benedictine Whipped Cream, for topping**

1. Rim a heated heat-resistant glass with demerara sugar.

2. Pour in En Fuego Potion (see recipe below) then ignite. Roll ignited potion in glass so that sugar rim starts to caramelize. For extra fun, put cinnamon in a powdered sugar shaker and shake over flame so that sparks fly.

3. Once the flame burns out, pour in Spanish Coffee Mix (see recipe below) and top with the whipped cream.

EN FUEGO POTION: Combine 1 part Bacardi 151 with 1 part Licor 43 and mix well.

SPANISH COFFEE MIX: Combine 2 oz. coffee, 1 oz. quality Spanish brandy, ½ oz. Amontillado sherry, ¼ oz. rich demerara syrup, and ¼ oz. Pedro Ximénez Sherry and mix well.

SALTED BENEDICTINE WHIPPED CREAM: In a bowl, combine 3 oz. heavy whipping cream, 1 bar spoon Madagascar vanilla bean paste, ¼ oz. rich demerara syrup, ¼ oz. Benedictine, and 2 drops saline solution (see page 47 for recipe) and whip together until stiff peaks form.

· EL NACIONAL ·

Mezcal and mole are a natural pairing that is complexly enhanced by the earthiness of the Ardbeg.

✦

GLASSWARE: Coupe

GARNISH: Lemon twist

- 1 oz. Del Maguey Vida Mezcal
- 1 oz. Campari
- ½ oz. Luxardo Amaro Abano
- ½ oz. dry vermouth
- 3 dashes mole bitters
- Ardbeg 5-Year Islay Scotch, for spritzing

1. Combine all of the ingredients, except the Ardbeg, in a mixing glass over ice, stir, and strain into a coupe.

2. Spritz with the Ardbeg and garnish with lemon twist.

· LOVE IN THE TIME OF COVID ·

"This cocktail was meant to be a one-off for a charity event during the Covid lockdown, but it became wildly popular, so much so that it became the first original cocktail on our menu. Previously we'd only done classics." —Keith Waldbauer

GLASSWARE: Cocktail glass

GARNISH: Lemon twist

- 1½ oz. Toki Japanese Whisky
- 1 oz. Lillet
- ¼ oz. Giffard Apricot Liqueur
- ¼ oz. Giffard Menthe de Pastille
- 2 dashes Peychaud Bitters

1. Combine all of the ingredients in a mixing glass filled with ice, stir, then strain into a chilled cocktail glass.

2. Garnish with a lemon twist.

LIQUID KITCHEN

KATHY CASEY

Seattle native Kathy Casey has been dubbed "America's First Bar Chef." She left home at the age of 14 to live in a convent, at one point even rooming with a retired bootlegger. By the time she was 26, she was the executive chef at Fuller's, a 5-star restaurant in downtown Seattle.

"There were no women chefs back then," she explains to me at her office in Ballard. "There were no women in fine dining, period—at least not in Seattle."

As her star rose, her story caught the attention of Craig Claiborne, the food and wine writer for the *New York Times*, who featured Kathy in a prominent article. "He was the godfather of food writers," she tells me. "It was a huge career blast. It was mind blowing."

In the decades since, she has traveled the world as a professional bar consultant, training bartenders in hospitality and creating cocktail programs for all sorts of clients, from small bars to cruise ships. "I create bars for people," she says. "I really love that."

In the 1980s, "I was going to Il Bistro a lot," she recalls. "I would sit at Murray's bar and drink cocktails. Everybody used to hang out at Murray's bar."

Back then—before the cocktail renaissance, during the period that Murray describes as "the nadir of drinking"—it was the disconnect between restaurants' food menus and their bar programs that inspired Kathy to help her clients merge them so they complement one another.

"Why weren't they using fresh juices?" she asks. "Why didn't cocktails feature ingredients from the food menu? Why not match the concept? Hello! Where do you think most of your money comes from? I wanted to bring principles from the kitchen into the bar."

When her friend and colleague Scott Staples opened Zoe in Bell-

town in the 1990s, Kathy offered to design the bar menu. Her touches brought the restaurant and bar instant success. "It became a slammin' busy bar," she says proudly. "It was crazy. It was very fun. Going into the 1990s, you started seeing bars use fresh juices, make craft margaritas. That's when we started seeing more interesting ingredients."

"It's all about technique and balance," she explains. "Technique and hospitality are key. If you order a martini and it arrives in a warm glass, or the vermouth has been sitting out, or the olives aren't chilled—these all have an effect." Kathy uses her expertise and experience to train bartenders and managers to avoid mistakes like these and focus on the guest experience. "What bothers me," she says, "is looking at a cocktail menu with too many ingredients, where I don't even know what half the stuff is. You look around—and these are cool places—and everyone is drinking wine. Why? Because the cocktails intimidate them. I think sometimes people let their egos get in the way of their cocktails."

• BLOODY SCANDI •

"Inspired by a trip to Portland, I combined House Spirits aquavit with Demitri's Bloody Mary Seasoning (a favorite bar staple from my longtime friend Demitri Pallis), a pinch of fresh dill, tomato juice, and garnished it up with all my favorite pickled things. As a Scandinavian, I personally would skewer some pickled herring too. If you prefer less aquavit in your drink, try substituting half of it for your favorite vodka."—Kathy Casey

GLASSWARE: Collins glass
GARNISH: Pickled beets, cucumber spear, other pickled items of your liking, fresh dill sprig

- 1½ oz. Krogstad Aquavit
- ¾ oz. Demitri's Extra Horseradish Bloody Mary Seasoning
- 4 oz. tomato juice
- 1 pinch chopped fresh dill

1. Build the cocktail in the Collins glass, fill with ice, and stir.

2. Garnish to your heart's desire.

· CRIMSON GARDEN ·

"**F**resh is always better. Try juicing at least three medium beets to make about a ½ cup of fresh juice. Elderflower or cucumber tonic is also delicious in this cocktail." —Kathy Casey

✦

GLASSWARE: Any fun glass
GARNISH: Thin slice of beet, edible rose petals

- 1½ oz. gin
- ½ oz. rose syrup
- 1 oz. fresh beet juice
- ½ oz. fresh lemon juice
- 1½–2 oz. Q Spectacular Tonic Water, chilled

1. Combine all ingredients in a cocktail shaker with ice, shake well, and pour into a glass.

2. Add tonic, stir, and top with more ice if needed.

3. Garnish with a thin slice of beet and edible rose petals.

• DOUGLAS FIR SPARKLE •

"This is absolutely my favorite cocktail for the Pacific Northwest. The light essence of Douglas fir infusing the gin evokes a truly local flavor. A splash of champagne adds festive bubbles. It is featured in the now iconic book, *What To Drink With What You Eat*, and was served at Seattle's Museum of History and Industry's Edible City Exhibit reception." —Kathy Casey

GLASSWARE: Cocktail glass
GARNISH: Tiny sprig of Douglas fir, fresh or frozen cranberry

- 1½ oz. Douglas Fir-Infused Gin
- ¾ oz. white cranberry juice
- ¾ oz. fresh lemon juice
- ¾ oz. simple syrup
- Splash of brut Champagne or sparkling wine

1. Combine all of the ingredients, except the Champagne, in a cocktail shaker with ice, shake well, and strain into a chilled cocktail glass.

2. Top with a splash of Champagne and garnish with a sprig of Douglas fir and a fresh or frozen cranberry.

DOUGLAS FIR-INFUSED GIN: Add 1 rinsed (5- to 6-inch) fresh-picked Douglas fir sprig to 1 (750 ml) bottle of gin and let stand for 24 hours; do not let it infuse for more than 24 hours. Remove the branch and discard. The infused gin can be stored at room temperature for up to one year. If fresh Douglas fir is not available, substitute a Douglas fir tea bag; if using the tea, add the contents of the tea bag to the gin, let infuse, and then strain the gin through a very fine strainer.

• BERRIES & BUBBLES •

"This cocktail celebrates lush Pacific Northwest raspberries, which, when in season, have an intoxicating flavor and aroma. You can find flower ice cube molds online."—Kathy Casey

GLASSWARE: Coupe

GARNISH: Edible organic flowers or a fresh raspberry, flower ice cube (optional)

- 3–4 fresh raspberries
- 1½ oz. vodka or gin
- ½ oz. simple syrup
- ½ oz. fresh lemon juice
- 1½ oz. brut Champagne or sparkling rosé

1. Combine all of the ingredients, except the Champagne, in a cocktail shaker with ice, shake well, and double strain into a chilled coupe.

2. Top with a splash of Champagne and garnish with edible flowers or a raspberry, and a flower ice cube, if desired.

• LIQUID KITCHEN OLD FASHIONED •

"This Old Fashioned gets a wonderful fragrance by smoking the glass over a burning cinnamon stick. I also enjoy it made with mezcal instead of cognac." —Kathy Casey

✦

GLASSWARE: Snifter

GARNISH: Wide orange peel, ice sphere, edible gold

- 1 cinnamon stick
- 1½ oz. bourbon
- ½ oz. cognac
- ¼ oz. rich demerara syrup
- 2 generous dashes Orange-Coffee Bitters

1. Using a torch, flame the end of a cinnamon stick inserted in a wood stave burning board; place a snifter over the smoking cinnamon stick.

2. Meanwhile, combine the remainder of the ingredients in a mixing glass with ice and stir until well chilled.

3. Remove the smoked glass from the burning board, place an ice sphere in the glass, and strain the cocktail over the ice.

4. Express the orange peel over the drink, twist, and add to the drink. Sprinkle with edible gold.

ORANGE-COFFEE BITTERS: Combine ¼ cup Angostura Bitters, 2 pieces of orange peel zest, and 8 espresso coffee beans in a bitters dasher bottle. Let infuse for 48 hours before using.

• HONEY MINT CARROT COLLINS •

"This garden-to-glass cocktail incorporates all the goodness, from honey to herbs to veggies. The carrot adds a subtle sweetness and a beautiful color, while playing well with the botanicals of the gin. If heirloom carrots are available at your farmers market, they make for a stunning carrot curl garnish." —Kathy Casey

GLASSWARE: Collins glass
GARNISH: Carrot curl (chilled in ice water), sprig of fresh mint

- 1½ oz. gin
- ¾ oz. Honey Mint Syrup
- ¾ oz. fresh carrot juice
- ¾ oz. fresh lemon juice
- 1–2 oz. chilled sparkling water

1. Combine all of the ingredients in a cocktail shaker with ice, shake well, and pour into a Collins glass.

2. Top the drink with the sparkling water and garnish with carrot curl and fresh mint.

HONEY MINT SYRUP: Combine 8 large sprigs fresh mint, ¾ cup clover honey, and ¾ cup water in a saucepan over medium-high heat and bring to a boil, stirring frequently. Once the mixture comes to a boil, reduce heat to low, and simmer for 1 minute. Remove from heat and let steep for 45 minutes. Strain and store refrigerated for up to 2 weeks.

• KATHY'S SPICED MANHATTAN •

"Liquid Kitchen spiced vermouths have become one of our bar staples. During the summer we use an infusion of blackberry, lemon, and spices, and in the fall it's an infusion of cranberry, clove, ginger, and orange. Stir these tasty, infused vermouths up in a Manhattan, or serve simply over ice." —Kathy Casey

GLASSWARE: Coupe
GARNISH: Wide orange peel, Amarena cherry (optional)

- 2 oz. bourbon or rye
- 1 oz. Liquid Kitchen Spiced Vermouth

- 2 dashes of your favorite bitters

1. Combine all of the ingredients in a mixing glass with ice, stir until well chilled, and strain into a chilled coupe.

2. If desired, garnish with a wide orange peel and Amarena cherry.

LIQUID KITCHEN SUMMER SPICED VERMOUTH*: Combine 2 cups sweet vermouth, 2 oz. spiced rum (or substitute white rum), 1 slice fresh ginger, 3 strips lemon peel, 10 fresh blackberries, 5 whole cloves, and 2 crushed allspice berries in a bottle and let infuse for a minimum of 3 days before using. Store refrigerated for up to 2 months.

*For a fall variation substitute the blackberries for cranberries and the lemon peel for orange

• HOLIDAY CRUSH •

"The best part about this cocktail is you can make it ahead of time. Make it with your favorite spirit then put a DIY spin on it by adding a handcrafted adornment or tag. This recipe yields enough for 8 (187 ml) bottles. The bottles are available online, as well as the metal caps and cappers. You can also find them at brewing supply stores." —Kathy Casey

---

◆

GLASSWARE: 187 ml bottles

- 1½ cups water
- ¾ cup sugar
- 2 cups vodka, gin, or blanco tequila
- ½ cup limoncello
- ½ cup pomegranate juice
- 1 cup fresh tangerine juice, or orange juice, fine strained
- ¾ cup fresh lemon juice, fine strained

1. Combine the water and sugar in a saucepan over medium-high heat and once the mixture boils, immediately remove from heat and cool to room temperature.

2. In a pitcher, combine the sugar syrup, spirit of choice, limoncello, and the juices and stir to combine.

3. Using a funnel, fill the bottles 1 inch from top; cap or seal. Store refrigerated for up to 2 weeks.

4. Serve cold; shake before serving.

• THE SMOKEY GREEN GODDESS •

"If you don't have a juicer at home, check out a local cold-pressed-juice shop for a juice with similar ingredients or experiment with new flavors." —Kathy Casey

◆

GLASSWARE: Old Fashioned glass
GARNISH: Cucumber curl or apple slice (optional)

- 1 oz. blanco tequila
- ½ oz. mezcal
- ½ oz. Monin Organic Agave Nectar
- ½–¾ oz. fresh lime juice, to taste
- 1 oz. Green Goddess Juice
- Tiny pinch of sea salt
- Garnish: cucumber curl or apple slice if desired

1. Combine all of the ingredients in a cocktail shaker with ice, shake well, and strain into an Old Fashioned glass over ice.

2. If desired, garnish with a cucumber curl or an apple slice.

GREEN GODDESS JUICE: Using a juicer, juice ½ bunch green kale, 1 large green apple, 1 cucumber, and 2 celery stalks, extracting as much juice as possible. Refrigerate in a jar for up to 2 days.

• BUZZED BUTTERED RUM •

"Traditionally mixed with hot water, this updated recipe uses hot coffee for a richer flavor, also adding a jolt of caffeine to get you through the gray days of Seattle winters. Make a batch of the buttered rum base to keep in the freezer for drop-in guests." —Kathy Casey

---

GLASSWARE: Coffee mug or snifter

GARNISH: Freshly grated nutmeg

- 1–1 ½ oz. aged rum
- 2–3 tablespoons Buttered Rum Mix
- 6 oz. hot coffee
- Lightly sweetened whipped cream, to top (optional)

1. Add the run and Buttered Rum Mix to a coffee mug, stir to combine, and then add the coffee.

2. Top with whipped cream if desired. Garnish with freshly grated nutmeg.

BUTTERED RUM MIX: In a bowl, combine 1 stick of room-temperature salted butter, ¾ cup packed brown sugar, ¾ cup powdered sugar, 1 ½ teaspoons very finely minced orange zest, 1 ½ teaspoons very finely minced lemon zest, ¾ teaspoon ground nutmeg, ⅛ teaspoon ground cloves, ¾ teaspoon ground cinnamon, and ⅛ teaspoon ground allspice and mix with an electric mixer on high speed for 5 minutes, until fluffy. Stop and scrape the bottom and sides of the bowl with a spatula. Add 1 cup softened vanilla ice cream and 1 ½ teaspoons vanilla extract and whip on medium-high for 90 seconds. Stop and scrape the bowl again, then whip on high for about 1 minute more, or until smooth. If the mixture looks broken, keep whipping; it will come together. The mix keeps, refrigerated, for up to 1 week or, frozen, for up to 2 months. If frozen, defrost before using.

THE NEXT GENERATION

POSTCARDS FROM NORWAY	CAFÉ OLD FASHIONED
REJECT IN THE ATTIC	SPICED PINEAPPLE DAIQUIRI
SAKE NIGHT IN CANADA	A PLETHORA OF PIÑATAS
ADRIELLE #2	A BREAK FROM GARDENING
TOO WEIRD TO LIVE, TOO RARE TO DIE	THE TRADEWINDS TAVERN ESPRESSO MARTINI
IT'S A WONDERFUL LIFE	GHOST IN THE SHELL
NEIL FROM YONKERS	TWO-TAILED FOX
THE SECRET GARDEN	EFFIE TRINKET
THE BLOOD IS LOVE	LYCHEE THIEVES
THREE GIRL RHUMBA	EMBERED LEMON
SIDECAR	THE GODFATHER
BAMBOO	BOILERMAKER
CHAMPS ELYSEES	THE DILL MURRAY
BRUNSWICK GARDENS	THE BOURBON BUZZER
KINGSLAYER	RAINIER MOSA
HIJINKS	OYSTER SHOOTER
BANK STATEMENT	TEA-INFUSED GIN AND TONIC
WHISPER IN THE WIND	THE SMOKED OLD FASHIONED
SHARPSHOOTER	'62 PANORAMA PUNCH
WITCH	SEATTLE HAZE
SCOTTISH LORE	SZECHUAN SOUR
HURT SO GOOD	PEAR-BERRY SANGRIA
FARMER'S ESTATE	YOU DO YUZU MOJITO
JOJO-NATIONAL	TROPICAL PARADISE
THE PORT OF NEGRONI	SEATTLE SOUR
THE FENNEL COUNTDOWN	PURPLE GIN FIZZ
	LYCHEE FIZZ MIMOSA

Now that Seattle is taken seriously as a cocktail juggernaut, what is the new class of drink slingers doing to keep the scene flourishing? Vegan bars, whiskey haunts, speakeasies, retro tiki joints, and an emphasis on local ingredients are some of the unique contributors from this Next Generation of Seattle bartenders.

LIFE ON MARS

KRAIG ROVENSKY, ANNIE LIFE, ALYCIA HYNES,
AND JENA MASON

"Life on Mars opened in the summer of 2019, which is like twenty years ago in pandemic times. We have lived and worked in Seattle for years, going to bars and restaurants and being a part of the music scene. As this city has changed, we wanted something that brought us back to the times when a neighborhood bar could be the place where you felt safe and in a community that wanted nothing more than great drinks, cozy atmosphere, and amazing music. We also wanted to make sure it had a plant-based menu as there are so few options available in Seattle. Our goal was not to open a bar just for vegans, but rather for those who will come to enjoy the drinks and music and discover that you can have brilliant food that doesn't involve meat or dairy. Our inspiration for the design came from a number of places: "old-school" Seattle, late-1970s New York City, and a healthy amount of time spent in Portland bars. We run a bar that we hope is unlike any other—supportive of its staff and never doing things the way they've always been done in this industry." —Kraig Rovensky

"**I** created Postcards from Norway in the fall of 2017 as a love letter of sorts—a love letter to three products that I felt would blend perfectly to encapsulate the feeling of receiving a postcard sent from a woman I loved." —Kraig Rovensky

✦

GLASSWARE: Coupe

GARNISH: Grapefruit twist

- 2 oz. Krogstad Aquavit
- ½ oz. Cardamaro
- ½ oz. Pierre Huet Pommeau de Normandie

- 2 dashes Miracle Mile Bitters
- Grapefruit twist, to express

1. Combine all of the ingredients, except the twist, in a mixing glass with ice, stir, and strain into a brandy snifter.

2. Express the grapefruit twist over the drink and discard.

· REJECT IN THE ATTIC ·

" **J**äger, polarizing, a reminder of bad college days. Why does it only ever get seen as such? Jägermeister is an amazing product to use behind the bar. So, wanting to prove that, and make a bitter cocktail for the amazing amaro bar that is Barnacle, I came up with this blend of bitter liqueurs for a menu in the spring of 2019." —Kraig Rovensky

◆

GLASSWARE: Collins glass

- 1 oz. Jägermeister
- 1 oz. Amaro Lucano
- ¾ oz. Cocchi Americano
- ¼ oz. Clear Creek Logan Berry Liqueur
- Q Grapefruit Soda, to top

1. Build in glass with ice, stir, and top with soda.

• SAKE NIGHT IN CANADA •

"**B**eing Canadian, this name has been stuck in my head forever. I made many different versions over the years before finally settling on this one. Creamy, light, and deceptive—I fell in love immediately. And I put it on the opening menu at Life on Mars in 2019." —Kraig Rovensky

GLASSWARE: Rocks glass

- 2 oz. sake
- ½ oz. Singani 63
- ¼ oz. Pierre Ferrand Dry Curaçao
- 1 oz. aquafaba
- ¾ oz. grapefruit juice
- ¼ oz. rich simple syrup
- A few dashes of Scrappy's Lime Bitters

1. Combine all of the ingredients, except the bitters, in a cocktail shaker with ice, shake well, and strain into a rocks glass over ice.

2. Finish with dashes of the bitters on top.

"**W**hen I ran Tavern Law I had the pleasure of working with Kory Snyder. He originally made this drink in 2017. I still think he was one of the city's finest drink makers. He had an incredible palate and could create amazing cocktails. Sadly, he was a man plagued with mental health problems, and addictions. Eventually those battles got the best of him and we lost him to suicide. I made this drink to honor him." —Kraig Rovensky

GLASSWARE: Rocks glass
GARNISH: Grapefruit zest

- ¾ oz. Banks 5-Year-Old Aged Rum
- ¾ oz. Avua Amburana Cachaca
- ¾ oz. Bruto Americano
- ½ oz. Giffard Pampelmouse
- ¾ oz. fresh lime juice
- ¼ oz. agave
- 1 egg white

1. Combine all of the ingredients in a cocktails shaker and shake well.

2. Add ice, shake again, and strain into a large rocks glass over ice.

3. Garnish with grapefruit zest.

• TOO WEIRD TO LIVE, TOO RARE TO DIE •

"**D**ave Flatman and I worked together at a bar called The Old Sage. One day while chatting, we both realized that we loved Branca Menta. So, we set about coming up with a drink with it. This was the result of that journey. A clear riff on a Last Word, it is weird but it will never die." —Kraig Rovensky

❖

GLASSWARE: Coupe

- ¾ oz. Del Maguey Vida Mezcal
- ¾ oz. Branca Menta
- ¾ oz. Luxardo Maraschino Originale
- ¾ oz. fresh lime juice

1. Combine all of the ingredients in a cocktail shaker with ice, shake well, and double strain into a coupe.

• IT'S A WONDERFUL LIFE •

This cocktail, created by Kraig Rovensky in late 2019, started its life as an Amaro Daiquiri and slowly turned into this full-on Amaro Sour. It's a delightful balance of floral, earthy, and citrus bitter flavors.

✦

GLASSWARE: Coupe

- ½ oz. Singani 63
- ½ oz. Amaro Lucano
- ½ oz. Amaro Amorino
- ½ oz. Small Hand Foods Orgeat
- ½ oz. fresh lime juice
- 1 oz. aquafaba
- A few dashes of Angostura Bitters

1. Combine all of the ingrdients, except the bitters, in a cocktai shaker with ice, shake well, and strain into a coupe.

2. Finish with a few dashes of bitters on top.

• NEIL FROM YONKERS •

❝I created this for the Life on Mars opening. One of the bar's most popular drinks, it has remained a top seller since day one. The Neil from Yonkers is a rich chai tea whiskey sour. And now that Townshend's is out of business, it's a limited-edition drink, because once we go through our very large back stock of Kashmir, it will be gone forever." —Kraig Rovensky

GLASSWARE: Coupe

GARNISH: Star anise pod

- 2 oz. Noble Oak Bourbon
- ½ oz. Townshend's Kashmiri Amaro
- ½ oz. fresh lemon juice
- ½ oz. rich demerara syrup

1. Combine all of the ingredients in a cocktail shaker with ice, shake well, and strain into a coupe.

2. Garnish with a star anise pod.

• THE SECRET GARDEN •

"Alicia Hynes and I met back in my Tavern Law days. She worked at the Mighty O Donuts on the corner, which was the closest spot for a quick coffee. We got to know each other over many months of me grabbing coffee. When we needed a new host at Needle and Thread, she was the first person who came to mind. A few years after leaving Tavern Law, when we were building out Life on Mars and I was thinking of staff, I called her to ask her if she wanted to come, and I am so glad she did. Alicia started here as a quiet barback who had a lot to learn. This was the first cocktail she made that I put on the menu, and remains to this day one of my all-time favorites." —Kraig Rovensky

---

GLASSWARE: Coupe

GARNISH: Edible flower

- 1 oz. Avua Amburana Cachaca
- ½ oz. Saint Benevolence rum
- ¾ oz. fresh lemon juice
- ½ oz. rich simple syrup

1. Combine all of the ingredients in a cocktail shaker with ice, shake well, and double strain into a coupe.

2. Garnish with an edible flower.

· THE BLOOD IS LOVE ·

"Throughout the three years that Life on Mars has been open, we have been blessed to have had bartenders with immense talents come through our doors. Zach Willet is one of those bartenders. Unfortunately for us, when Covid happened Zach and his lovely wife moved to Portland. We can't say enough how we miss his dancing and goofy antics behind the bar." —Kraig Rovensky

GLASSWARE: Coupe

- 1½ oz. Bently Heritage Juniper Grove Gin
- 1½ oz. Bitter Nardini
- ½ oz. green Chartreuse

1. Combine all of the ingredients in a mixing glass with ice, stir, and strain into a coupe.

· THREE GIRL RHUMBA ·

"**W**hen we opened back up in the post Covid-lockdown world and started working on cocktails again, Jena Mason became obsessed with making drinks with Jäger. She tried dozens of versions, even using coconut yogurt at one point (It was . . . okay). But I never stopped believing that she would nail it. So, when we were putting out the winter menu at the tail end of 2020 I told her I was committed to helping her find something that would not only work, but be super badass. This is that cocktail. Jena has been at Life on Mars since day one, coming on as a server, and eventually becoming GM."—Kraig Rovensky

GLASSWARE: Coupe

- ¾ oz. Père Labat 59 Rhum Agricole
- ½ oz. Lairds Apple Brandy
- 1 oz. Jägermeister
- ¾ oz. Bittermens Tepache
- ¼ oz. Small Hand Foods Passion Fruit Syrup

1. Combine all of the ingredients in a mixing glass with ice, stir, and strain into a coupe.

THE FAIRMONT OLYMPIC HOTEL

JESSE CYR

Jesse Cyr started working in hospitality when he left his acting career in Los Angeles and moved to Seattle. Ready for a fresh start, he landed a job at Rob Roy, an internationally acclaimed bar in Seattle's Belltown neighborhood. He was eventually promoted to general manager and opened their newest venture, Navy Strength. When he left the company, Jesse began working at a brand-new downtown spot called The Charter Hotel. As beverage director, he operated the rooftop bar, Fog Room, and created the cocktail menus for their Argentinian restaurant, Patagon. His resume also includes working at James Beard nominated French restaurant and natural wine bar, L'Oursin, and the infamous cocktail lounge, Foreign National. Jesse has been fortunate enough to consult on cocktail development for well-known brands like Beam/Suntory, Campari America, Lucas Bols, and Torani Coffee, to name a few. Currently, Jesse is the beverage director at the Fairmont Olympic Hotel and oversees all four bars at the location.

"I think Seattle gets a bit overlooked compared to other big cities," he tells me. "But it's really on par with the rest of the major urban areas in terms of cocktails and bars. There's a very large diversity in guests that come into your bar, whether from the tourism industry, business travel, or the ever-changing Seattle tech landscape. It's fun to hear everyone's story and what they're all about. Plus, we've got a pretty tight-knit bar community and we look out for each other. It's always great to go out and know you'll run into someone who will know your name."

• SIDECAR •

"The Sidecar is in the top three of my favorite cocktails. I really believe that it's one of the most underrated classic cocktails out there because of how many variations there are that deviate from the original recipe. When perfectly balanced with a solid cognac and high-quality orange liqueur, this drink sings beautifully. And in case you're wondering, there's no need for a sugar rim. Ever." —Jesse Cyr

GLASSWARE: Coupe

- 2 oz. VSOP Cognac
- ¾ oz. Grand Marnier
- ¾ oz. fresh lemon juice
- 1 bar spoon rich demerara syrup

1. Add all of the ingredients to a cocktail shaker with ice, shake well, and strain into a coupe.

• BAMBOO •

"The Bamboo is a great cocktail option for when you want to drink, but also want to take it easy. Just because you want a low ABV beverage doesn't mean you need to make a sacrifice when it comes to flavor. The sherry blend in this Bamboo is key to achieving a great depth and complexity." —Jesse Cyr

GLASSWARE: Nick and Nora glass

GARNISH: Lemon twist

- 1½ oz. dry vermouth
- ¾ oz. Amontillado Sherry
- ½ oz. Fino sherry
- ¼ oz. Lustau East India Solera Sherry
- 1 bar spoon simple syrup
- 2 dashes Angostura Bitters
- 2 dashes orange bitters

1. Add all of the ingredients to a mixing glass with ice, stir, and strain into a chilled Nick and Nora glass.

2. Garnish with a lemon twist.

• CHAMPS ELYSEES •

" **I** credit this cocktail with getting me into bartending. The Champs Elysees was the first real cocktail I ever experienced. I was living in Los Angeles and a friend took me to The Varnish, an incredibly well-respected and proper cocktail bar. No sweet and sour, no mixers from a gun. It was just high-quality ingredients crafted to perfection. From that day on, I knew I wanted to make drinks like that." —Jesse Cyr

❖

GLASSWARE: Coupe

GARNISH: Lemon twist

- 2 oz. VSOP Cognac
- ¾ oz. fresh lemon juice
- ¼ oz. Green Chartreuse
- ¼ oz. simple syrup
- 2 dashes Angostura Bitters

1. Add all of the ingredients to a cocktail shaker with ice, shake well, and fine strain into a coupe.

2. Garnish with a lemon twist.

• BRUNSWICK GARDENS •

"**M**y first bar job in Seattle was at Rob Roy and this cocktail was the first drink I ever got to put on their menu. I was so happy to be learning and working at such a well-known bar, and to finally have something I created on their menu was very exciting for me. This cocktail turned into one of their best sellers. A cucumber and lavender sour? What's not to love?" —Jesse Cyr

GLASSWARE: Sour glass

GARNISH: Cucumber wheel, pink Himalayan sea salt

- 2 cucumber wheels
- 1 ½ oz. London dry gin
- 1 oz. fresh lemon juice
- ½ oz. Lavender-Lemon Syrup
- 1 egg white

1. Break up the cucumber wheels into quarters and place them in a cocktail shaker. Add the rest of the ingredients and shake hard without ice for 10 to 15 seconds.

2. Add ice to the shaker, shake again, and then fine strain into a sour glass.

3. Garnish with a thin cucumber wheel floated on the foam and dust with the sea salt.

LAVENDER-LEMON SYRUP:
Peel 3 lemons with a y-peeler. In a small saucepan, combine the peels and 2 ½ tablespoons dried lavender with 2 cups water and bring to a boil. Reduce heat and simmer for 20 minutes. Add 2 cups sugar and stir until completely dissolved. Remove the pan from the heat, let steep for 15 minutes, and then fine strain through cheesecloth; discard the solids. Bottle, refrigerate, and use within 3 weeks.

• KINGSLAYER •

"This cocktail is a mash-up of a Sazerac and a Manhattan. Opting for a lighter-bodied cocktail, the blanc vermouth brings a nice roundness and herbaceous flavor that pairs nicely with the bitter Cio-Ciaro. Instead of rinsing the glass with absinthe, just a bar spoon of its less potent cousin, pastis, brings a wonderful bright note to the finish."
—Jesse Cyr

GLASSWARE: Rocks glass

GARNISH: Lemon twist

- 1½ oz. Eagle Rare 10 Bourbon
- 1 oz. Dolin Blanc Vermouth
- ½ oz. CioCiaro Amaro
- 1 bar spoon pastis
- 2 dashes Peychaud's Bitters

1. Add all of the ingredients to a mixing glass with ice, stir, and strain into a chilled rocks glass.

2. Garnish with a lemon twist.

"Single malt Scotch drinkers seem to rarely mix their whiskey, so this cocktail is a little nod to showing them that they can relax a bit and have some fun with it. No need to be so serious! The delicate floral aromas from the chamomile and fino sherry really help to create a unique flavor profile that is definitely nontraditional of single malt Scotch cocktails." —Jesse Cyr

❖

GLASSWARE: Coupe
GARNISH: Dehydrated lemon wheel

- 1½ oz. Glenmorangie X
- ¾ oz. Lustau Fino Sherry
- ¾ oz. Chamomile Syrup
- ½ oz. fresh lemon juice

1. Add all of the ingredients to a cocktail shaker with ice, shake well, and strain into a coupe.

2. Garnish with a dehydrated lemon wheel.

CHAMOMILE SYRUP: Bring 2 cups water to a boil and then pour into a heatproof container. Add 3 chamomile tea bags and steep for 10 minutes, agitating every few minutes. Remove tea bags, add 2 cups white cane sugar, and stir until dissolved. Let cool and refrigerate; use within 10 days.

• BANK STATEMENT •

"While working at a rooftop bar, I knew that whatever vodka cocktail I put on the menu was going to be the top seller. So, I really leaned into hitting all the notes that one expects from vodka cocktails on a roof in the middle of the summer: bright, fruity, tart. Plus, topping it off with sparkling rosé? You can't go wrong!"
—Jesse Cyr

✦

GLASSWARE: Coupe

GARNISH: Edible violet flower

- ¾ oz. vodka
- ¾ oz. Dolin Blanc Vermouth
- ½ oz. Lychee Rose Tea Syrup
- ½ oz. fresh lemon juice
- 1½ oz. sparkling rose

1. Add all of the ingredients, except the rosé, to a cocktail shaker with ice, shake well, and fine strain into a coupe.

2. Add the sparkling rosé and garnish with an edible violet flower.

LYCHEE ROSE TEA SYRUP: Add 2 cups water to a saucepan and bring to a simmer. Remove the pan from heat, add 4 tablespoons loose-leaf lychee rose tea, stir to combine, and steep for 10 minutes, stirring occasionally. Fine strain through cheesecloth and return the tea to the saucepan. Add 1 ½ cups sugar and stir until dissolved. Let cool and refrigerate; use within 10 days.

• WHISPER IN THE WIND •

" **I** originally made this cocktail for the Bols Around The World global competition in 2016. I ended up getting second place in the States that year and I wanted to have this drink on a menu, but it really didn't fit with where I was working at the time. Two years after the fact, the Whisper in the Wind finally made its official debut on a Seattle cocktail menu. To this day, this drink is the one that I'm most proud of creating." —Jesse Cyr

◆

GLASSWARE: Sour glass

- 1½ oz. Bols Genever
- ¾ oz. Acid Adjusted Orange Juice
- ½ oz. Lillet Rosé
- ¼ oz. Giffard Apricot Liqueur
- ¼ oz. simple syrup
- 1 egg white

1. Add all of the ingredients to a cocktail shaker and shake for 10 to 15 seconds.

2. Add ice to the cocktail shaker, shake well, and fine strain into a sour glass.

ACID ADJUSTED ORANGE JUICE: This recipe requires that all of the ingredients are measured on a scale. In a bowl, combine 500 grams of strained orange juice, 12½ grams citric acid, 10 grams malic acid, and 5 grams orange blossom water and stir to incorporate. Bottle, refrigerate, and use within 3 days.

• SHARPSHOOTER •

❝In an episode of *The Great British Baking Show*, one of the hosts mentioned how lavender and blackberry was a delicious combination. I thought to myself that those flavors would pair really well with a smoky mezcal. It worked seamlessly! Mezcal has such an array of flavors to it, depending on which agave species is used. I highly recommend using an arroqueño or madre-cuishe if you can afford it. Otherwise, an espadin is absolutely acceptable." —Jesse Cyr

◆

GLASSWARE: Collins glass

GARNISH: Mint sprigs

- 1½ oz. mezcal
- ¾ oz. fresh lemon juice
- ½ oz. crème de cassis
- ½ oz. Honey Syrup
- 2 dashes lavender bitters

1. Build the ingredients in a collins glass and then fill the glass two-thirds full with pebble or crushed ice. Use a swizzle stick to mix.

2. Top with more ice until full and garnish with 2 or 3 mint sprigs.

HONEY SYRUP (YIELDS 1½ CUPS): Add 1½ cups honey to a heat-resistant container and then add ¾ cup hot water. Stir until the water is fully incorporated and a consistent texture is achieved. Let cool, refrigerate, and use within 10 days.

ROB ROY, MBAR

JOJO KITCHEN

"My first time working behind a bar was at Forrest Point in Bushwick, Brooklyn," explains Joanna "Jojo" Kitchen. "It was a neighborhood restaurant that had an awesome cocktail program. It was where I learned how to make Milk Punch and where I learned to shake a cocktail. I met amazing humans there who inspired me to become a bartender."

She began as a barback, and later moved up to bartending for weekend brunches. "Shortly after, I moved to Seattle, trading in the concrete jungle for the Pacific Northwest," she says.

In 2018 she landed a job barbacking at The Fog, a high-end rooftop cocktail bar. "In two months I was bartending and the rest is history."

She has since tended bar at Aerlume and No Anchor, and currently whips up delicious cocktails at Mbar and Rob Roy.

• WITCH •

"This is one of the first cocktails I created at Fog Room. Once I was introduced to Strega there it really started my love affair with amaro. I wanted to make a cocktail with all my favorite ingredients, cinnamon syrup, tequila and Strega. An experiment gone right."
—Jojo Kitchen

✦

GLASSWARE: Double Old Fashioned glass
GARNISH: Lemon twist

- 1½ oz. blanco tequila
- ¾ oz. Strega Amaro
- ¾ oz. fresh lemon juice
- ½ oz. cinnamon syrup

1. Combine all of the ingredients in a cocktail shaker with ice, shake well, and double strain into a glass over a large ice cube.

2. Garnish with lemon twist.

"This was created for one of my favorite regulars at Rob Roy. It's awesome when you work at a bar that gives you a platform to make bespoke cocktails, where the customers come in knowing what kind of bar they are at and want a bartender's choice. My favorite thing to hear is "Make me whatever you want, I trust you." The original name of this cocktail was The Ayuba Special." —Jojo Kitchen

❖

GLASSWARE: Double Old Fashioned glass
GARNISH: Lemon twist

- 1½ oz. Oban 14
- ½ oz. Ardbeg Corryvreckan
- ¼ oz. Benedictine
- ¼ oz. CioCiaro Amaro
- Barspoon of rich simple syrup
- 4 dashes Angostura Bitters

1. Combine all of the ingredients in a mixing glass with ice, stir lovingly for 30 seconds, and strain into a glass over a large, hand-cut ice cube.

2. Garnish with a lemon twist.

• HURT SO GOOD •

"This cocktail was created at Mbar for a Negroni week special. It's a tropical old pal riff." —Jojo Kitchen

✦

GLASSWARE: Nick and Nora glass

GARNISH: Lemon twist

- 1 Pineapple-husk infused cap course
- 1 oz. mezcal
- ¾ oz. Campari

1. Combine all of the ingredients in a mixing glass with ice, stir lovingly for 30 seconds, and strain into the glass.

2. Garnish with a lemon twist.

• FARMER'S ESTATE •

" **I** wanted to make a cocktail that was sourced from local ingredients, something that showcases all of the amazing flavors of the Pacific Northwest. One of my favorite things about Seattle summers is the farmers markets. Late summer you can find honeydew melon and amazing peaches and nectarines. A true patio crusher with bright botanicals." —Jojo Kitchen

GLASSWARE: Rocks glass
GARNISH: Sage leaf

- 1¾ oz. Big Gin Infused with Honeydew
- ¼ oz. Clear Creek Pear Brandy
- ¾ oz. fresh lemon juice
- ½ oz. E9 Farmhouse Ale Syrup made with farmers market peaches
- 4 dashes Yuzu bitters

1. Combine all of the ingredients in a cocktail shaker with ice, shake well, and double strain into a glass over a large ice cube.

2. Garnish with lemon balm leaf.

• JOJO-NATIONAL •

"This is a shot I make at Mbar all the time. It's festive and once someone sees it, everyone wants one. The build is a shot for two because no one should take a shot by themselves. After the past two years we should all celebrate life and indulge in a fun shot once in a while." —Jojo Kitchen

GLASSWARE: Shot glasses

- 1½ oz. Plantation Stiggins Rum
- ½ oz. Giffard Apricot Liqueur
- 1 oz. pineapple juice
- ½ oz. fresh lime juice
- ¼ oz. simple syrup
- 4–5 dashes Peychaud's Bitters, to top

1. Combine all of the ingredients in a cocktail shaker with ice, shake well, and fine strain into two shot glasses.

2. Top with bitters.

THE SPIRITS IN MOTION

JASON ANDERSON

In 2012, Jason Anderson became the sous chef, cocktails-on-tap specialist, and beverage program developer for Kathy Casey, and now manages beverage innovation for national accounts at The Spirits in Motion. For more than two decades he has developed beverage programs, created cocktail recipes, trained bartenders, designed draft cocktail systems, and helped to open more than 200 bars and restaurants globally. From luxury hotels to national chains, cruise ships, movie theaters, and food and beverage conferences, Jason has been a part of it all. He has a passion for all things beverage and finds his skills in the kitchen priceless when applying them to beverage development. "The best part about the food and beverage industry is that you never stop learning," he says. "There are always new techniques to be discovered, and I believe it is my responsibility as a teacher never to stop learning. When you think that you've figured it all out, that is the time you need to hang up your apron, pack up your tools, and clock out for the last time."

• THE PORT OF NEGRONI •

" **N**egronis are delicious! There is no doubt about that. This one, is remixed with the addition of tawny port wine. Tawny port's mandarin orange, fig, and caramel notes perfectly complement the bitter orange flavors of Campari and the botanical nature of gin." — Jason Anderson

✦

GLASSWARE: Coupe

GARNISH: Flamed orange peel disk

- 1 oz. OOLA Gin
- 1 oz. Campari
- 1 oz. tawny port wine

1. Combine all of the ingredients in a mixing glass with ice, stir, and strain into a coupe.

2. Flame the orange disk over the drink and drop it into the glass.

• THE FENNEL COUNTDOWN •

"**I** feel like fennel and Chartreuse are long lost brothers, and this combination showcases that. Add in a touch of celery, bright lime juice, barrel-finished gin, sugar, a hint of orange, and you are in business." —Jason Anderson

◆

GLASSWARE: Double Old Fashioned glass
GARNISH: Lime wheel, fennel frond

- ½ oz. Fennel-Infused OOLA Vodka
- 1 oz. OOLA Barrel-Finished Gin
- 1 bar spoon green chartreuse
- ½ oz. dry curaçao
- ¾ oz. fresh lime juice
- ½ oz. simple syrup
- 3 drops celery bitters
- 1½ oz. Q Spectacular Tonic Water

1. Combine all of the ingredients, except the tonic, in a cocktail shaker with ice, shake well, and strain over fresh ice into a double Old Fashioned glass.

2. Garnish with lime wheel and fennel frond.

FENNEL-INFUSED OOLA VODKA: Slice 1 fennel bulb into strips and add them and the fronds to a large glass jar with a lid. Add 1 (750 ml) bottle of OOLA Vodka to the jar, seal it, and infuse for 3 days, shaking every day. Strain and refrigerate for up to 3 months.

• CAFÉ OLD FASHIONED •

"**B**ourbon and coffee have been going steady for some time now, and they still love each other. For good measure, I threw in some nutty spice notes, aromatic bitters, orange oil, and finished it all off with a bittersweet chocolate snack to enjoy with this delicious concoction." —Jason Anderson

GLASSWARE: Double Old Fashioned glass
GARNISH: Wide orange peel, coffee beans, dark chocolate square

- 2 oz. OOLA Waitsburg Bourbon
- ¼ oz. coffee liqueur
- 1 bar spoon demerara syrup
- 3 dashes Fee Brothers Black Walnut Bitters
- 1 dash Angostura Bitters

1. Combine all of the ingredients in a mixing glass with ice, stir, and strain into double Old Fashioned glass over a large square ice cube.

2. Express orange peel over the drink, twist, and drop it in the glass. Top with coffee beans and serve a chocolate square on a plate next to the cocktail.

• SPICED PINEAPPLE DAIQUIRI •

"The daiquiri is one of my favorite cocktails, and I feel that it is the perfect drink to make when trying a new rum. The Spiced Pineapple Daiquiri is an easy one to make, and will please even the harshest critic of rum." —Jason Anderson

GLASSWARE: Coupe

GARNISH: Lime wheel, freshly grated nutmeg

- 1½ oz. Bacardí Reserva Ocho Rum
- ½ oz. Plantation Stiggins' Fancy Pineapple Rum
- ¾ oz. fresh lime juice
- ¼ oz. pineapple juice
- ½ oz. simple syrup
- 3 dashes Angostura Bitters
- 1 pinch cinnamon

1. Combine all of the ingredients in a cocktail shaker with ice, shake well, and strain into a coupe.

2. Float lime wheel on cocktail and top with freshly grated nutmeg.

• A PLETHORA OF PIÑATAS •

" *Three Amigos* is one of my favorite movies, and if given the chance, I would make El Guapo this cocktail as a birthday gift. Spicy, fruity, citrusy, and fun. If only I could serve it in a piñata without it spilling." —Jason Anderson

✦

GLASSWARE: Double Old Fashioned glass
GARNISH: Strawberry Pop Rocks for rim, lime wedge, strawberry

- 1 strawberry, sliced
- 1½ oz. Tres Agaves Organic Blanco Tequila
- ½ oz. Ancho Reyes Ancho Chili Liqueur
- ¼ oz. Cointreau
- 1 oz. fresh lime juice
- ¾ oz. agave

1. Rub the lime wedge garnish along the upper ½ inch of a double Old Fashioned glass, dip the glass in Pop Rocks, and set aside.

2. Add the sliced strawberry to a cocktail shaker and lightly muddle.

3. Add the remainder of the ingredients to the cocktail shaker with ice, shake well, and strain into the prepared glass over fresh ice.

4. Garnish with lime wedge and strawberry attached to rim of glass.

• A BREAK FROM GARDENING •

" **N**ot all cocktails need booze. Arguably, they are better with it, but this one lacks nothing. It is herbal, vegetal, bright, and bubbly. A perfect beverage to enjoy while taking a break from gardening. Throw in some alcohol—1½ oz. vodka or gin and cut down on the soda—if the weeds get the better of you." —Jason Anderson

GLASSWARE: Collins glass

GARNISH: Long rosemary sprig (6 inches), cucumber wheel

- 3 slices of English cucumber
- 1 oz. fresh lemon juice
- 1 oz. simple syrup
- 3 oz. soda water

1. Add the cucumber slices to a cocktail shaker and lightly muddle.

2. Add the lemon juice and simple syrup to the cocktail shaker with ice and shake well.

3. Add soda water to the shaker and pour into a Collins glass; add more ice if necessary.

4. Tuck the rosemary sprig into the glass and top with the cucumber wheel.

TRADEWINDS TAVERN

CUYLER HARRIS

Raised in the South and now flourishing in the Pacific Northwest, Cuyler Harris has been behind the stick for over a decade at dive bars, fancy Rum bars, and 4-star hotels, and is now running some of Seattle's finest bar programs (Rob Roy, et al.), He loves a good pour of mezcal and a spicy amario, or an over-the-top, very-much-on-fire tropical beverage rich with complexities and garnishes.

"To me, hospitality has always been about treating people with courtesy and respect in an individualized fashion. It's about making every interaction with a guest unique to their 'vibes' and fostering a fun, non-pretentious environment where everyone can exist. Repetitive, rehearsed service speeches have never been my thing and frankly are insulting to the guest who is very often looking for a personalized experience. There is an immense deal of sensitivity, active listening and on-the-spot evolution necessary when reading a guest and attending to their needs, especially the ones who maybe aren't having the best day. To me, it is vital to focus on and turn those people's experiences around, maybe it's something personal they're going through or maybe they had a terrible experience at another bar. I just love doing something special and intentional for someone and having them feel seen; that is all anyone wants, really.

"Seattle has been very kind to me over the years, in no small way attributed to the warmth and generosity of the hospitality industry. Known for its contributions to the global conversation about crafting cocktails, and being a prominent figure in the resurgence of Prohibition Aged Cocktails, Seattle feels like entering a hallowed hall of immeasurable talent and opportunity. Many of the bars I've had the privilege to work in in Seattle feel more like Shaolin Temples, where I can hone my skills in the same rooms as these indomitable figures, all

the while becoming more disciplined and centered in my craft. Being a creative bartender in Seattle has some real, undeniable bucket list energy to it. "This city has always been wildly diverse, and it remains an artists' playground. There is no shortage of inspiration and *no* substitution for that crackling energy you feel when you walk into the right cocktail bar. I remain ever humbled and grateful for my time spent here."

Espresso martinis are making a resurgence in Seattle, and bar guests expect excellence. Tradewinds' version lives up to those expectations, thanks to how the sweetened condensed milk balances out the pleasant bitterness of a quality cold brew coffee.

◆

GLASSWARE: Nick and Nora glass
GARNISH: 3 coffee beans

- ¾ oz. vodka
- 1 oz. cold brew coffee
- 1 oz. Mr. Black Coffee Liqueur
- ¼ oz. sweetened condensed milk

1. Combine all of the ingredients in a cocktail shaker with ice, shake well, and fine strain into a Nick and Nora glass.

2. Garnish with three coffee beans.

• GHOST IN THE SHELL •

❝I made this one when I was the bar manager of Brunswick & Hunt up in Ballard between 2015 and 2019, a cute little family-owned bar with a restaurant attached. I had carte blanche over the whole menu and always rotated seasonal stuff in and out. I was able to play with a lot of beautiful ingredients and really stretch my legs, creatively speaking. This is easily one of the most popular cocktails I ever created and it became a mainstay on the menu year round. It's spicy and refreshing, with a hint of nutty, sweet smoke and a big herbaceous backbone. I was honored when it was featured on the Friends & Family menu in 2018 at Teardrop Lounge, an amazing little cocktail bar in Portland, Oregon." —Cuyler Harris

◆

GLASSWARE: Collins glass

GARNISH: Several sprigs of mint

- 1 oz. Del Maguey Vida Mezcal
- 1 oz. Amontillado sherry
- ¾ oz. fresh lime juice
- ½ oz. orgeat
- ½ oz. ginger syrup (1:1 sugar to ginger juice)

1. Combine all of the ingredients in a cocktail shaker with ice, shake well, and double strain into the glass.

2. Top with crushed ice and garnish with mint.

"This one I made during my tenure at Rob Roy. After a significant restructuring, this cocktail was first featured on the winter menu even though it was really more of spring sipper. I wanted to create something that was refreshing enough to be enjoyed on a hot summer day, but also something spirit forward that could be sipped slowly and wasn't the same old tall, fruit-juice refresher, margarita, or daiquiri riff that one might see on a typical menu. It's definitely boozy bastard, but also finely complex with moscat-forward Bolivian brandy as the base, and the more floral blanc vermouth balances the dryness. Not a lot of people may know how perfect of a pairing of allspice and brandy can be, but I think that's one of the key elements to this drink. And that little pop of citrus bitters brings up the acid without introducing, or diluting the spirits to hell with juice. It made some rounds in the cocktail circuit and is potentially my opus as a barman. Unfortunately, only three months after debuting this menu at Rob Roy, the pandemic hit and everything shut down. Tragically, this drink hasn't been sipped enough by the undoubtedly clamoring masses." —Cuyler Harris

❖

GLASSWARE: Double Old Fashioned glass
GARNISH: Dehydrated lime wheel

- 1½ oz. Singani 63 Bolivian Brandy
- ¾ oz. Dolin Blanc
- ¼ oz. Pierre Ferrand Curaçao
- ¼ oz. Del Maguey Vida Mezcal
- ¼ oz. St. Elizabeth Allspice Dram
- 2–3 dashes Scrappy's Bergamot Bitters

1. Combine all of the ingredients in a mixing glass with ice, stir lovingly for 30 seconds, and strain into a glass over a large, hand-cut ice cube.

2. Garnish with a dehydrated lime wheel.

RUMBA

JEN AKIN

Jen Akin grew up on a hobby farm in Lawrence, Kansas. She started her career in hospitality working at The Replay Lounge, an infamous Midwest dive bar, then worked her way through college at University of Missouri, Kansas City, slinging drinks at beer bars, Irish pubs, and Mexican cantinas, perfecting her Guinness pours and scratch margaritas. She went on to work at 715, where she fell in love with cocktails and became enamored with spirits.

After graduating, Akin moved to Seattle to attend medical school at UW, and began bartending at the downtown Local 360. Soon, as her passion for spirits and cocktails developed, she decided to put medical school on hold and leap headfirst into the bartending world. Akin joined the United States Bartenders Guild, worked at Oliver's Twist, Tavern Law, and Needle & Thread, and designed her first bar program for Alchemy at The Winchester Inn in Ashland, Oregon. She then assumed the role General Manager at her dream bar, Rumba in the Capital Hill neighborhood. In her five years there, she garnered multiple accolades including three nominations from Tales of the Cocktail Spirited Awards for World's Best Spirits Selection, Best Bar-West, and Best Bar Team-West. Most recently, Akin and her Rumba team opened Inside Passage, a Pacific Northwest-inspired underwater immersion bar.

Her current loves include Daiquiris, specifically ones made with KoHana rum; painting; and her three dogs Taco Dumpling, Swizzle Stick, and Augy Doggy.

The peppery lemongrass notes of the Ten to One White Rum are beautifully balanced out by the syrup and orange flower water in this drink.

✦

GLASSWARE: Collins glass

GARNISH: Mint bouquet

- 1½ oz. Ten to One White Rum
- ¾ oz. Ferrand Pineau des Charentes
- ¾ oz. jasmine syrup
- ¾ oz. fresh lemon juice
- 2 dashes orange flower water

1. Build the drink in the glass over crushed ice and swizzle to combine.

2. Garnish with mint bouquet.

· LYCHEE THIEVES ·

Colorful, fragrant, fresh, this drink is the tropics in a glass.

GLASSWARE: Collins glass
GARNISH: Lychee, edible orchid

- ¾ oz. Rhum J.M Blanc 55%
- ¾ oz. Byrrh Grand Quinquina Liqueur
- ¾ oz. Giffard Lichi-Li
- ¾ oz. fresh lime juice
- ¼ oz. rich simple syrup
- 1½ oz. ginger beer, to top

1. Combine all of the ingredients, except the ginger beer, in a cocktail shaker with ice, shake well, and strain into a glass over ice.

2. Top with ginger beer and garnish with lychee and an orchid.

COLLEGE CLUB OF SEATTLE

JESSE STANG

Jesse Strang is a native Seattleite who began his bartending career in Beppu, Japan. While attending university there, he and his schoolmates decided to open a bar for the international students. Beppu Social Bar was a huge success and quickly became a staple of the local night life.

Jesse returned to America in 2018 and began working for The College Club of Seattle, building the food and beverage program to the point that it became known far and wide.

• EMBERED LEMON •

"I came up with this drink at one of our dock concerts at the College Club. I am a huge fan of Luxardo maraschino cherries, and the syrup—I put a tiny splash of it in my Manhattans too. I was out of cherries and I did not want the syrup to go to waste, so I decided to make a cherry lemonade with the best ingredients. This mix goes well with vodka, gin, or whatever you like. My preference is a quality mezcal like Del Maguey Vida. I try to always shake my drinks with the fruit in, rather than muddling. This allows the flavor profile to express itself to the fullest without bruising the fruit." —Jesse Stang

GLASSWARE: Rocks glass

- 1½ oz. mezcal
- 1½ oz. fresh lemon juice
- ¾ oz. Luxardo Maraschino Cherry Syrup
- 2 Luxardo Maraschino Cherries

1. Combine all of the ingredients in a cocktail shaker with ice, shake well, and strain into rocks glass over ice.

· THE GODFATHER ·

" **I** created this drink variation when I was bartending in Japan at a bar my friends and I opened named Beppu Social Bar (BSB). It is one of my go-to drinks. However, when I order it at most places, it is way too sweet. I have even observed bars and online recipes use a 1:1 ratio of Disaronno and Scotch. It is my humble opinion that those bartenders are sent to a special place in hell. I decided to perfect the ratio with the best ingredients while still keeping it simple. I love this drink because it has complex undertones while still simple and packing a punch. When a Scotch on the rocks is just a little too heavy, a light dash of amaretto and the refreshing citrus of an orange peel really softens the bite." —Jesse Stang

GLASSWARE: Rocks glass

GARNISH: Orange peel

- 2¼ oz. Balvenie 12
- ¼ oz. Disaronno Originale
- Orange Peel garnish

1. Build the drink in a rocks glass over ice.

2. Express orange peel over the drink and then add the peel to the drink.

EMERALD CITY COCKTAILS

NEIL RATLIFF

So much of what is written about bartending regards hallowed brick and mortar establishments and cutting-edge chemistry—but little is spoken about the chaos and excitement of event bartending.

In 2016, I quit my gig at Blueacre Seafood in Seattle and flew to Denver, Colorado, to tour the workshop of Customized Designs, crafters of portable event bars. I used my savings to buy one of their custom setups and launched Emerald City Cocktails, a professional bartending service for parties, weddings, and corporate gatherings in the Pacific Northwest. Like Demitri Pallis, I found himself surrounded by equipment in a cramped one-bedroom apartment in West Seattle, working toward a dream: providing an elevated level of service and cocktail quality for pop-up bars at parties.

In no time, I was hiring my bartender friends to keep up with demand, as we executed events for cannabis brands, rustic weddings, spirit marketing—really every kind of celebration imaginable. In 2019, we opened for business in Oregon, and the following year expanded to San Francisco and Los Angeles. Emerald City Cocktails is now the largest professional bartending service on the West Coast.

I was so nervous before my first event in 2016 that I was unable to sleep the night before. Now we crush up to thirty events per week. Bar catering was stale when we started. Now wedding guests expect cocktails good enough to splash all over Instagram, and companies want to provide employees with elevated, enjoyable experiences.

My favorite quote about business is from Warren Buffett: "No company ever went bankrupt by wowing their clients."

• BOILERMAKER •

A staple of the Seattle happy hour. Pour a shot of OOLA Waitsburg bourbon and serve with a tall boy of Rainier or Olympia beer.

• THE DILL MURRAY •

This recipe was my first ever entry in a cocktail competition. I did not win, but I absolutely love it. Why is dill not used more often? It has a cool, refreshing, crispness to it, which plays great with spicy firewater bitters and sparkling brut. There is a painting in the Chicago Art Institute nicknamed "The Bill Murray Painting," named so because of a famous Bill Murray story. After a disastrous performance early in his career, Bill was so overwhelmed with disappointment that he listlessly wandered the streets of downtown Chicago. As the sun rose, he found himself in front of the Chicago Art Institute and, directionless, went inside. He came upon a painting that struck a chord—a woman tending a field with the sun rising behind her. He credits the painting with his decision to pick himself up and keep moving forward with performing. I think of this story anytime I'm questioning myself.

GLASSWARE: Collins glass
GARNISH: Dill sprig

- **Dill sprig**
- **2 oz. OOLA Gin**
- **¾ oz. cucumber juice**
- **½ oz. agave nectar**
- **½ oz. fresh lime juice**
- **3 dashes Scrappy's Firewater Bitters**
- **Domaine Ste. Michelle Brut, to top**

1. Muddle the dill in a cocktail shaker, then add all of the ingredients, except the brut, with ice, shake well, and strain into a Collins glass over ice.

2. Fill the glass with Domaine Ste. Michelle Brut and garnish with dill sprig.

• THE BOURBON BUZZER •

This cocktail is in line with Seattle's unofficial mantra "put coffee in everything." The cold brew cuts down on the oaky bite of bourbon and the orange from the Grand Marnier plays well.

GLASSWARE: Collins glass
GARNISH: Coffee beans

- 1¼ oz. OOLA Waitsburg Bourbon
- ¾ oz. Grand Marnier
- 2½ oz. cold brew coffee
- 1 oz. organic maple syrup
- 2 dashes orange bitters
- Cream of choice, to float

1. Combine all of the ingredients, except the cream, in a cocktail shaker with ice, shake well, and strain into a Collins glass.

2. Float cream on top and garnish with several coffee beans.

· RAINIER MOSA ·

Fancy cocktails are great, the best really, but there is much to be said for a cheap, cold drink, Seattle style.

◆

GLASSWARE: Pint glass

GARNISH: Orange wheel

• **2 oz. fresh orange juice**　　• **12 oz. Rainier Beer**

1. Add the orange juice to a frosted pint glass, fill the glass with cold Rainier Beer, and garnish with an orange wheel.

• OYSTER SHOOTER •

The salty waters of the Pacific Northwest yield an abundance of wild and farmed oysters like Kumamotos, Virginicas, Pacifics, and Olympias (the only native species) that are most delicious shucked and sucked down. But if you're going to add something to a raw oyster, why not make it a shot?

✦

GLASSWARE: Shot glass

- Demitri's Rim Shot
- 1 shucked oyster
- 1 oz. chilled vodka
- 1 oz. Demitri's Bloody Mary Mix

1. Rim a chilled shot glass with Demitri's Rim Shot and add a shucked oyster.

2. Add the vodka and Demitri's Bloody Mary Mix to the glass and enjoy.

DEMITRI'S BLOODY MARY MIX: Mix 1 part Demitri's Bloody Mary Seasoning with 3 parts tomato juice.

• TEA-INFUSED GIN AND TONIC •

I t's easy to infuse gin, and if you take the time to do it, you'll be that much closer to being able to pour simple beauty into a glass at a moment's notice.

✦

GLASSWARE: Old Fashioned glass
GARNISH: Edible flower

- 2 oz. Suntory Roku Gin Infused with Hibiscus Tea
- Tonic, to top

1. Pour the infused gin into an Old Fashioned glass over ice, top with tonic, and garnish with a fresh edible flower.

SUNTORY ROKU GIN INFUSED WITH HIBISCUS TEA: Add several buds of hibiscus tea to a 750 ml bottle of Suntory Roku gin and let stand for 24 hours. Strain and store.

• THE SMOKED OLD FASHIONED •

RAVIN BUZZELL

How do you add a new dimension to a classic? Pull out the smoking gun!

GLASSWARE: Rocks glass

GARNISH: Lemon swatch

- 2 oz. rye
- ½ oz. simple syrup
- 3 dashes cardamom bitters
- Cherrywood chips

1. Using a smoking gun, fill a glass decanter with cherrywood smoke and put a lid on it.

2. Combine all of the ingredients in a mixing glass with ice, stir, and strain into the smoke-filled decanter. Cover and swirl to incorporate the smoke.

3. Pour the drink into a rocks glass over a king cube and garnish with a lemon swatch.

•'62 PANORAMA PUNCH •

INSIDE PASSAGE

At Inside Passage, this drink is served in an actual 1962 Seattle World's Fair glass. Let this fruit and spice creation transport you to the World of Tomorrow.

◆

GLASSWARE: Collins glass
GARNISH: Bay leaf, candied cranberries,
scoop of mandarin-almond sorbet

- 1 oz. Trois Rivières Amber Rum
- ½ oz. Rhum Clément Creole Shrubb
- ½ oz. Copperworks Gin
- ½ oz. fresh lime juice
- ½ oz. cranberry juice
- 1½ oz. mandarin-almond sorbet

1. Combine all of the ingredients in a cocktail shaker with ice, shake well, and strain over ice into a collins glass.

2. Garnish with bay leaf, candied cranberries, and scoop of mandarin-almond sorbet.

· SEATTLE HAZE ·

NICOLE STANKOVIC, EMERALD CITY COCKTAILS

Don't let the name fool you, this bright cocktail will shine through any haze.

GLASSWARE: Coupe

GARNISH: Grapefruit slice

- 1½ oz. mezcal
- ½ oz. Grand Marnier
- ½ oz. Aperol
- ¾ oz. fresh lemon juice

1. Place all of the ingredients in a cocktail shaker with ice, shake until chilled, and strain into a coupe.

2. Garnish with a grapefruit slice.

• SZECHUAN SOUR •

Nicole Stankovic's mother has owned the award-winning Szechwan Chinese Kitchen in Park City, Utah for over thirty years, which is how Nicole first got into bartending. Szechuan peppercorns are used in a variety of dishes at the restaurant to create floral notes and tingling sensations, so Nicole made sure they found their way onto the specialty cocktail menu at Emerald City Cocktails.

GLASSWARE: Cocktail glass
GARNISH: Szechuan peppercorns

- 2 oz. whiskey
- 1 oz. fresh lemon juice

- 1 oz. Szechuan Peppercorn-Infused Simple Syrup
- 1 large egg white (optional)

1. If using egg white, place all of the ingredients in a cocktail shaker without ice and shake for 60 seconds. Add ice to the shaker and shake again for 30 seconds. Strain into a cocktail glass and garnish with Szechuan peppercorns.

2. If not using egg white, place all of the ingredients in a cocktail shaker with ice, shake until chilled, and strain into the cocktail class; garnish with Szechuan peppercorns.

SZECHUAN PEPPERCORN-INFUSED SIMPLE SYRUP: Grind 1 tablespoon Szechuan peppercorns. Dissolve ½ cup sugar in ½ cup boiling water, remove from heat, add ground peppercorns, and steep for 20 minutes. Strain and store in an airtight container.

• PEAR-BERRY SANGRIA •

This riff on a classic brightens up even the gloomiest of days.

GLASSWARE: Wine glass

GARNISH: Blackberries, orange slices

- ½ lemon, sliced thin
- Juice of ½ lemon
- ½ orange, sliced thin
- Juice of ½ orange
- 8 blackberries
- 1 Asian pear, cored and diced
- 2 oz. brandy
- 2 oz. Grand Marnier
- 2 oz. sugar
- 1 (750 ml) bottle of dry red wine
- 1 cup ginger ale

1. Muddle the fruit and juices in a large pitcher.

2. Add the brandy and Grand Marnier to the pitcher and mix well. Wait 10 minutes before adding the sugar and wine. Mix well.

3. Cover and refrigerate for at least 4 hours.

4. When ready to serve, add ginger ale and stir. Garnish with blackberries and orange slices.

• YOU DO YUZU MOJITO •

Yuzu sake is a relatively new development on the drinks scene, but it is a welcomed one.

◆

GLASSWARE: Highball glass
GARNISH: Mint sprigs

- • Sugar, for the rim
- • ¼ oz. simple syrup
- • ½ lime, quartered
- • 6–8 mint leaves
- • 5 oz. yuzu sake
- • Club soda, to top

1. Wet the rim of a highball glass and dip it into the sugar.

2. Place the simple syrup and lime quarters into the glass and muddle.

3. Smack, twist, and drop the mint leaves into the glass and add ice.

4. Add the yuzu sake, top with club soda, and stir.

5. Garnish with a few mint sprigs.

• TROPICAL PARADISE •

If you don't have a cocktail umbrella on hand, fear not. The aroma of coconut cream is sure to take your mind to the tropics, no matter where you're sipping this one.

GLASSWARE: Rocks glass

GARNISH: Dried or fresh pineapple slice, cocktail umbrella

- 1½ oz. tequila
- ½ oz. coconut cream
- ½ oz. simple syrup
- ½ oz. orange juice
- 1 oz. pineapple juice
- 1 dash Angostura Bitters

1. Place all of the ingredients in a cocktail shaker with ice, shake well, and strain into a rocks glass.

2. Garnish with a dried or fresh pineapple slice and a cocktail umbrella.

• SEATTLE SOUR •

EMERALD CITY COCKTAILS
NEIL RATLIFF

I love this drink. Instead of a small red wine float like a New York Sour, pour a few fingers of a local pinot noir on top. Drinking with and without a straw provides two totally different flavors

✦

GLASSWARE: Rocks glass
GARNISH: Luxardo cherries

- 2 oz. OOLA Waitsburg bourbon
- 1 oz. fresh lemon juice
- 1 oz. simple syrup
- Oregon pinot noir, to float

1. Fill a rocks glass with ice.

2. Add all of the ingredients, except the wine, to a cocktail shaker, shake well, and strain into the rocks glass, leaving a wash line of 1 to 2 inches.

3. Float the wine on top and garnish with Luxardo cherries.

• PURPLE GIN FIZZ •

Antioxidant-rich butterfly pea flower tea has long been popular for its health benefits, but its stunning color has made it a favorite ingredient among bartenders looking to make a drink that is equal parts delicious and eye-catching.

◆

GLASSWARE: Rocks glass
GARNISH: Basil sprig

- 1 oz. Purple Basil Syrup
- 1 oz. fresh lemon juice
- Club soda

- Butterfly Pea Flower Tea-Infused Suntory Roku Gin

1. Fill a rocks glass with ice.

2. Add the Purple Basil Syrup and lemon juice to a cocktail shaker, shake wall, and strain into the rocks glass.

3. Fill the glass with soda, leaving a wash line of 1 inch.

4. Float the infused gin on top of the cocktail and garnish with sprig of basil.

PURPLE BASIL SYRUP: Mix 1 cup water with 1 cup sugar and bring to a boil. Add 10 purple basil leaves and reduce to a simmer for 10 minutes. Let cool, strain, and store.

BUTTERFLY PEA FLOWER TEA-INFUSED ROKU GIN: Add 10 butterfly tea flowers to ¼ liter gin, seal, and let steep overnight. Strain and store.

• LYCHEE FIZZ MIMOSA •

The traditional mimosa is good, but not exciting, unlike this beautifully perfumed cocktail.

◆

GLASSWARE: Collins glass
GARNISH: Lychee

- 1 oz. lychee syrup
- ½ oz. rose water

- Sparkling rosé

1. Fill a Collins glass with ice, add the lychee syrup and rose water, fill the glass with sparkling rosé, and stir.

2. Garnish with lychee fruit.

OOLA OLD FASHIONED

PERFECT GIN GIMLET

THE GREAT HOUDINI

OOLA LA G&T

THREE SHORES SAZERAC

TAKE ME TO THE RIVER

THE BLACK LODGE

THE METRÓPOLI

AÑEJO NEW FASHION

BLACKBERRY MINT MARGARITA

WATERMELON JALAPEÑO MARGARITA

SCRATCH BACON BLOODY MARY

(OR CAESAR)

GAME DAY MARY

SMOKIN' MARY

MOSCOW MULE

DARK AND STORMY

We make everything we need right here in the Emerald City! Bourbon, tequila, ginger beer, salmon-safe whiskey, cocktail ice, and the perfect Bloody Mary mix are just some of the local ingredients you will find here in Seattle.

OOLA DISTILLERY, ELECTRIC CELLO, AND 10 DEGREES

KIRBY KALLAS-LEWIS, ALAN JACKSON, KT NIEHOFF, AND JASON ANDERSON

Kirby Kallas-Lewis is likely not who you have in mind when you envision a master spirits maker. He is tall and thin—not bearded and burly—and he is jolly, inviting, and generous. He was born in St. Paul, majored in sculpture and fine art in college, and after school he hitchhiked to Alaska to work on fishing boats. From there, he purchased a one-way ticket to the South Pacific and spent the next two decades exploring the region. He is considered one of the world's most important dealers of South Pacific antiquities. In 2008, he bought a still and set it up in his bathtub; within two years, he founded OOLA Distillery, Seattle's oldest maker of spirits.

"We like to say that our product is 'Artfully Distilled,'" explains Alan Jackson, OOLA's managing director, as he shows me around their operations plant in the industrial SODO district just south of downtown. They use low-yield yeast, which reduces their output but produces a better-tasting product. Alan explains that they distill "on the grain," meaning that the grain is not separated before fermentation, adding to the texture and the flavor of their spirits. Their bourbon is made using a stainless pot still, and aged in barrels for five and a half years—the longest aging processes of any bourbon made in Seattle—at a facility next to a Buddhist monastery (which Alan credits for an infusion of positive vibes into the barrels). For their gin, Kirby adorns a white lab coat and adds a proprietary blend of thirteen botanicals to their neutral vodka spirit, creating a wonderful New-World-style product that makes an incredible Gin and Tonic. All of their spirits are organic and certified salmon-safe (a peer-reviewed certification that implements business practices that protect water quality and habitats in the name of preserving Pacific salmon), and they recently installed a closed-loop water cooling system that now saves them tens of thousands of gallons of water per year.

"Electric Cello is an intimate, 44-seat bar and restaurant that focuses on OOLA Distillery spirits and pairing craft cocktails with locally sourced, hyper-seasonal food," explains proprietor KT Neihoff, who partnered with Kirby Kallas-Lewis from OOLA for the project. With longtime Seattle chef Aaron Wilcenski in the kitchen, they take great care to pair the food with OOLA's spirits, working with the gin botanicals, curing fish in gin, and building garnishes for the cocktails.

"Electric Cello, OOLA Bottle Shop, and 10 Degrees are about unearthing and elevating cocktail and food pairings for everyone to experience," KT continues. "They are also about the constant search for why gathering in public spaces matters."

10 Degrees is a space for events, art, performance, and community gatherings in the heart of the Georgetown neighborhood. "I want it to be the church of Georgetown," says Kirby as he shows me around.

KT talks about the importance of the location for the venue. "The ethos of Georgetown is blue collar, tattoos, and counterculture. It is a little lawless, a little Bourbon Street, and a little bad kid. Like the East Village in New York, the Tenderloin in San Francisco, and the Marais in Paris—all of these micro-neighborhoods are interesting because they retain and honor their roots. People visit these neighborhoods to be immersed in their unique energy."

• OOLA OLD FASHIONED •

"The preconceived notion that all Old Fashioneds have to be made with whiskey is a bunch of B. S. Delicately balancing the vanilla-infused honey juniper tones of OOLA's Barrel-Finished Gin with orange bitters and lemon zest brings this cocktail to life! A perfect alternative to the classic brown spirit drink." —Kirby-Kallas-Lewis

✦

GLASSWARE: Double Old Fashioned glass
GARNISH: Wide lemon peel

- 2 oz. OOLA Barrel-Finished Gin
- 1 bar spoon simple syrup
- 2 dashes orange bitters

1. Combine all of the ingredients in a mixing glass with ice, stir, and strain into a double Old Fashioned glass over a large square ice cube.

2. Express the lemon peel over the drink, twist, and drop into the glass.

• PERFECT GIN GIMLET •

"Gimlets are the OG citrus gin cocktail. Gins should always be tasted by themselves, and then immediately made into a gimlet to get the full spectrum of flavors. We make ours with fresh lime and occasionally add a chili pepper float—a classic culinary comrade for fresh lime. No cordial needed here."—Kirby Kallas-Lewis

GLASSWARE: Coupe

GARNISH: Lime peel, herb sprig of choice

- 2 oz. OOLA Gin
- ¾ oz. fresh lime juice
- ½ oz. simple syrup

1. Combine all of the ingredients, in a cocktail shaker with lots of ice, shake well, and strain into a coupe.

2. Express the lime peel over the drink, discard, and garnish with fresh herb sprig

· THE GREAT HOUDINI ·

"**C**ocktails should be entertaining! The Great Houdini is magical, colorful, and refreshingly delicious. The balance of citrusy vodka, color changing lavender syrup, lemon juice, and bubbly soda water is all brought together with the interactive swoosh of rosemary to mix up all of the fun, and unexpected color surprise." —Kirby Kallas-Lewis

GLASSWARE: Collins glass

- **1 long rosemary sprig (5–6 inches)**
- **1½ oz. OOLA Citrus Vodka**
- **1 oz. lavender butterfly syrup**
- **1½ oz. soda water**
- **¾ oz. fresh lemon juice**

1. Place the rosemary sprig in a Collins glass and then build the drink, without adding the lemon juice, and stir.

2. Add ice to fill the glass 1 inch from the rim and then slowly float lemon juice on top of the cocktail.

3. Grab the rosemary sprig and bob it up and down, mixing lemon juice thoroughly and changing the drink's color.

· OOLA LA G&T ·

"**G**in and tonics have exploded in popularity over the past decade. They range from simple gin and tonic water to a complex layering of multiple ingredients. We chose the balanced middle ground for ours, with botanical OOLA Gin, bright lime, a touch of sugar, and good quality tonic water. The garnish choice is all yours. Go crazy!"—Kirby Kallas-Lewis

GLASSWARE: Wine glass

GARNISH: Bartender's choice (edible flower, cucumber slices, lime wheel, fresh herbs, juniper berries, etc., etc.)

- 1½ oz. OOLA gin
- ½ oz. fresh lime juice
- ½ oz. simple syrup
- 2 oz. Q Spectacular Tonic

1. Build drink in the glass, stir, and add ice to fill the glass.

2. Garnish lavishly—this cocktail is a blank canvas, so paint it with love.

• THREE SHORES SAZERAC •

"The Sazerac was originally invented in New Orleans, but we took a global approach to this delicious cocktail. OOLA's Discourse Three Shores Whiskey is a combination of our American high-rye Waitsburg Bourbon, Highland Scotch, and Canadian whiskey. No matter which way you look at it, our Sazerac competes with the best of them."—Kirby Kallas-Lewis

✦

GLASSWARE: Rocks glass
GARNISH: Lemon peel

- ½ bar spoon absinthe in glass
- 2 oz. OOLA Three Shores Whiskey
- ¼ oz. simple syrup
- 3 dashes Peychaud's Bitters

1. Add the absinthe to the glass, swirl it around, pour it out, and set aside the glass.

2. Combine the remainder of the ingredients in a mixing glass with ice, stir, and strain into the prepared glass.

3. Express the lemon peel over the cocktail and attach it to the rim of the glass.

• TAKE ME TO THE RIVER •

"The Pacific Northwest has a lot of Scandinavian influence, and this cocktail pays homage to that culture through the combination of OOLA's London dry juniper-forward gin, Brovo's herbaceous vermouth, and a touch of Krogstad's anise- and carraway-forward aquavit."—Kirby Kallas-Lewis

GLASSWARE: Coupe
GARNISH: Sweety Drop Pepper

- 3 oz. OOLA ALOO Gin
- ¼ oz. Brovo Witty Dry Vermouth
- 1 bar spoon Krogstad Aquavit
- Lemon peel disk

1. Combine all of the ingredients, except the lemon peel, in a mixing glass with ice, stir, and strain into a coupe.

2. Express the lemon peel over the drink, discard, and drop pepper into the glass so it sinks.

• THE BLACK LODGE •

"This is our truly unique Pacific Northwest version of a black Manhattan. The buttery oak, maple, and caramel toffee notes in our Waitsburg Bourbon Whiskey plays beautifully with the bitter vanilla chocolate and savory rhubarb characteristic combination of Highside's Amaro Mele, and Fast Penny's Americano Amaro."—Kirby Kallas-Lewis

GLASSWARE: Coupe

GARNISH: Wide orange peel

- 2 oz. OOLA Waitsburg Bourbon Whiskey
- ½ oz. Highside Amaro Mele
- ½ oz. Fast Penny Amaricano Amaro

1. Combine all of the ingredients in a mixing glass with ice, stir, and strain into a coupe.

2. Express the orange peel over the drink and drop in, or attach to the rim of the glass.

COPPERWORKS DISTILLERY

JASON PARKER

Jason Parker met me at his distillery in Pike Place Market one afternoon to show me around and tell me the story of Copperworks. I interrupted his lunch, and I told him that I had plenty of time and to please enjoy his meal. "No, I'm good!" he exclaimed as he popped up from his desk and enthusiastically shook my hand. He mentions that he's from Kentucky, and I excitedly told him that my family was, too.

"How did you make it all the way out here to Seattle?" I ask.

"I ran out of land getting away from Kentucky," he jokes.

Graduating from Evergreen College after studying chemistry and microbiology, Jason founded the iconic Pike Brewery in the Market in 1989.

"From great brewing comes great spirits," he tells me. The local brewing community came together organically, he explains, with a "really good camaraderie." He used his brewing knowledge to open Copperworks some years later, with the goal of making high-quality beer, then distilling it. "We are brewers first," he says. "I think brewers and distillers will be interchangeable in fifty years."

"We have never made a decision based on inefficiency," he goes on. "For a distillery, starting with beer is inefficient. It's all about flavor, not yield."

Sourcing their ingredients from local breweries—Pike, Elysian, and Fremont, to name a few—they distill fermented grain and age the spirits in oak barrels.

"We didn't need to be traditional," explains Jason, "and that also means removing traditional impurities from our spirits."

Copperworks takes a vintage approach to their whiskey-making, meaning they source single-farm malt to infuse individual characteristics to their batches, much like grapes to a winery.

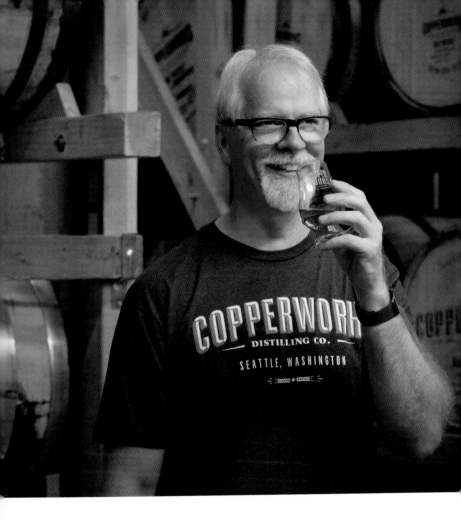

"Whiskey is the perfect product for malt!" Jason exclaims.

Their Batch 39 Whiskey was the first such spirit to be certified salmon-safe, and like OOLA they have installed a towered water-cooling system that now saves them tens of thousands of gallons of water in the production process.

BLACK ROCK SPIRITS

SVEN LIDEN

I first met Sven Liden at my company's five-year anniversary party, when we rented the Tequila Lab office near Seahawks stadium to host the event. The creaky wooden building that houses the Black Rock Spirits headquarters is over a hundred years old, compartmentalized into artist lofts. Sven met me downstairs to let me in so I could set up for the party, and we started talking shop, chatting about booze, bartending, and the old-school office.

"You know, this room was Nirvana's first practice space," Sven said nonchalantly.

"What? That's awesome! Our event tonight is a 1990s-themed costume party, how fitting."

"Cool," he said. "Would you guys want to try some of our tequila tonight?"

Yes we would, I nodded. Yes we would.

With his partner, Chris, Sven started Black Rock Spirits in 2008. The first product they sold was a bottle of Bakon, a bacon-infused vodka designed for use in a Bloody Mary.

"We realized that as a small company, it's very difficult to achieve the reach that big spirits brands get by spending millions of dollars on marketing," says Sven. "Our strategy has been to produce very high-quality products, but to market the bottles and brands in ways that get attention just from the name or label. But, with Bakon, instead of going for novelty, we decided to use all-natural ingredients and a high-quality potato base. In the last decade it's won countless national awards for Best Bloody Mary.

"Most of the time when you are introduced to a new spirit it's because a big company paid a distributor sales rep to introduce the product to a bartender, even paid to print their menus and featured

cocktail lists," Sven goes on. "They throw around a lot of money to push awareness of a new brand. We have always been focused on a 'pull' versus 'push' strategy. We started off with a really attention-getting product, Bakon Vodka. But our next product, Sparkle Donkey Tequila, was also meant to get attention with unique and funny branding, including a fake documentary about the history of El Burro Esparkalo, a donkey that came down the hillside to deliver tequila to a town in need. We use very high-quality ingredients and traditional cooking and distillation methods. We work with a boutique distillery in the town of Tequila, Mexico, to make a 100-percent agave tequila without using diffusers or taking shortcuts. Our Silver tequila was rated 93 points and we've won a number of gold medals in international competitions, typically beating out tequilas that are twice our retail price. Our customers may first sample Sparkle Donkey because of the irreverent branding, but then they become fans because of the great taste and quality. "

· THE METRÓPOLI ·

"**P**eople often think of tequila for summer cocktails, but reposado tequilas are a great substitute for whiskey in cocktails that you might enjoy in the fall or winter. The Metrópoli is similar to a Manhattan but uses Sparkle Donkey Reposado." —Sven Liden

✦

GLASSWARE: Cocktail glass
GARNISH: Orange zest and/or brandied cherry (optional)

- 2 oz. Sparkle Donkey Reposado
- 1 oz. sweet vermouth
- 1 dash orange bitters

1. Combine all of the ingredients in a mixing glass with ice, stir well, and strain into a chilled cocktail glass.

2. If desired, garnish with orange zest and/or a brandied cherry.

• AÑEJO NEW FASHION •

The story of the Sparkle Donkey—or El Burro Esparkalo as he is better known—began as little more than a local anecdote about a humble-yet-noble creature that, in dire times, delivered liquid salvation to many who were in need. But as time passed and word of his strange, lustrous aura and invigorating, ambrosial drink spread, the Sparkle Donkey became a powerful symbol of hope.

GLASSWARE: Old Fashioned glass

GARNISH: Orange twist

- 2 oz. Sparkle Donkey Añejo
- ½ oz. simple syrup
- 2 dashes Angostura Bitters
- 2 dashes orange bitters
- 1 dash vanilla extract

1. Combine all of the ingredients in a mixing glass with ice, stir well, and strain into the glass.

2. Garnish with an orange twist.

• BLACKBERRY MINT MARGARITA •

" For a refreshing summer cocktail (although they are great any time of year!) it's fun to just add an additional ingredient or two to the standard margarita." —Sven Liden

❖

GLASSWARE: Rocks glass

GARNISH: 2 blackberries skewered on a pick

- 6 blackberries
- 1½ oz. Sparkle Donkey Reposado
- 1 oz. fresh lime juice
- 1 oz. simple syrup or agave
- 10 mint leaves

1. Place the berries in a cocktail shaker and muddle them, then add ice and the remainder of the ingredients, shake well, and pour into a rocks glass.

2. Garnish with 2 blackberries skewered on a pick.

• WATERMELON JALAPEÑO MARGARITA •

❝The combination of sweet and hot in a margarita is delicious! I often like to make 'low carb' versions of this by substituting monk fruit drops or erythritol or allulose syrup for the simple syrup."
—Sven Liden

✦

GLASSWARE: Rocks glass
GARNISH: Jalapeño slices, watermelon slice

- 3 jalapeño slices
- 2 oz. watermelon
- 2 oz. Sparkle Donkey Silver tequila
- 2 oz. watermelon juice
- 1 oz. fresh lime juice
- 1 oz. simple syrup

1. Place the jalapeño and watermelon in a cocktail shaker and muddle them, then add ice and the remainder of the ingredients, shake well, and pour into a rocks glass.

2. Add a few slices of jalapeños to the glass and garnish with a watermelon slice.

DEMITRI'S BLOODY MARY SEASONING

DEMITRI PALLIS

Seattle native Demitri Pallis grew up in Rainier Beach. He invites me into the upstairs office of his warehouse in Georgetown, where a drum kit takes up most of the back corner. The first thing I want to know is what it was like growing up in Seattle in the 1980s. "Pioneer Square was fun," he says. "It was joint cover night—you would pay the bouncer in joints for the cover charge and you would get into all the bars. This is before Belltown, before Ballard, even before Capitol Hill really popped. Between the clientele and the substances that were rolling around at the time, Pioneer Square was a hot mess."

"That sounds pretty rad," I say.

He chuckles. "Oh yeah, it was fun."

In 1983, Demitri started his career at Jake O' Shaughnessy's, a bar and restaurant in the Queen Anne neighborhood that boasted the Guinness World Record for Largest Collection of Spirits. "It wasn't fancy back then," he explains. "Every now and then you would get someone to make you a nice cocktail—a Ramos Fizz, Tequila Sunrise, Mai Tai, or Slippery Nipple—not like now." He worked there for several years, crediting the training he received for his passion and success today. "I loved making nice drinks and doing it well. I loved getting my eyeball measurements, my eyeball pours. When I'm done shaking it's to the drop, right where it's supposed to be. I really like making complicated drinks."

He left Jake's in 1986 to tend bar at The New Orleans Creole Cafe, which had a slightly different training policy than he was accustomed to. "It was a rolling train wreck at all times," he says. "My first day, the owner tossed me the keys and said, 'If you have a problem, you deal with it.'" He found the lack of standards frustrating,

but does admit that it was liberating to have the freedom to do whatever he wanted.

"Everyone was ordering drinks differently. They called drinks by different names. They wanted me to make drinks differently for them. I said, no the drink is made this way. I told the owner, 'Hey, at the next meeting, I have some ideas about how we can shape up and streamline everything.'"

"We don't have meetings," the owner responded. "They just cause problems."

It was during his time at the New Orleans that he confronted the problem he would dedicate the rest of his life to solving: making enough of the perfect Bloody Mary mix, and making enough of it before a bar shift.

"I said to myself, this is a nightmare. This one drink is the death of me. If I made too much, it would spoil. If I didn't make enough, we would run out before a Seahawks game. I would go from selling $7 Bloody Marys to $2 longnecks and it just crushed my ring out."

His new colleagues avoided the task, or concocted mixes that were too spicy or too boring, and the onus fell on him to make a tasty batch that would get them through a long brunch.

"At the time, even now, a lot of people were unfamiliar with how to create a base like that," he explains. "I fiddled with the recipe for about a year, so the ratio would come out tasting right. Pretty soon, the guys at The Central and Merchant's Cafe and those places said 'Hey, mix me some of that shit, I hate making Bloody Marys!'"

"I thought, you know what? I'm going to call some people."

He brought a sample to his uncle, who owned a bar in the nearby South Lake Union neighborhood, and the feedback was positive. Customers loved it, his uncle reported, and bartenders did too as it was simple to make. "This really makes sense!" the uncle exclaimed in his Greek accent. Demitri, aware that he was onto something, got to work.

"I lived above Romeo's Pizza on Interbay for about five years. My first pallet of plastic bottles showed up and the trucker was laughing at me. I had to carry a hundred and something cases up my stairs. My roommate was a little miffed when he came home."

Seattleites are famous for starting successful businesses in their garages; Demitri launched his empire from his apartment, punching in for long bar shifts at The New Orleans and then coming home to work on his new project until sunrise. His mixes that today sell in bars and restaurants in all fifty states have a humble beginning.

"I remember working until 3 or 4 in the morning all the time. Hand delivering. I'd put all the stuff in my powder-white 1966 Chrysler Valiant. Someone had broken off my antenna to make a crack pipe, so I had a coat hanger on there. I've had spills, giant spills, in my apartment. I had a 55-gallon drum and I'd mix the stuff with a Craftsman drill."

"There is no such thing as 'the best Bloody Mary.' The Bloody Mary is probably the only drink you can make countless different ways, and still call it a Bloody Mary. Same goes with garnishes. I know it's boring, but I actually don't mind celery in my Bloody Mary. For me, the garnish is really the extension of the drink. If it's a Bloody Mary with fresh dill and lemon, a cucumber spear or wheel might work better than a fried chicken wing. That said, a spicy wing is always nice with a well-spiced Mary. I've had versions by other names with gin instead of vodka, Irish whiskey, and even rum. All well made and tasty! Adding a dash of orange juice or grapefruit juice is also a tasty variation. Leave an inch at the top and fill with a nice nutty porter. Drip a little sticky balsamic vinegar down the inside of the glass for a fun visual and a sweet tang. For all of these reasons, and so many more, when people ask me for some of my favorite drink or garnish recipes, I'm never quite sure what to say. But here's a crack at it."

• SCRATCH BACON BLOODY MARY • (OR CAESAR)

"Bakon Vodka will help you make the best Bloody Mary you've ever had. It has a strong smoky and savory profile with lots of umami notes, and that flavor comes through even in a cocktail as complex as a Bloody Mary or Caesar. So even if you use your favorite mix or concentrate and just add Bakon Vodka, it will take the cocktail to a new level. And, if you're going through the trouble of making a round of Bloody Marys for a brunch for your friends, it's worth the extra effort to have fun with the garnishes. A slice of bacon, a few chicken wings on a skewer, cheese blocks, or even a slider on a skewer will make for an amazing boozy brunch showcase."—Demitri Pallis

GLASSWARE: Salt-rimmed pint glass
GARNISH: Celery stalk, pickled vegetables, etc.

- 1½ oz. Bakon Vodka in a pint glass filled with ice.
- Tomato juice (or Clamato for a Caesar)
- 1 dash celery salt
- 1 dash black pepper
- 2–4 dashes Worcestershire sauce
- 2–4 dashes Tabasco

1. Add the vodka to a mixing glass filled with ice, pour in enough tomato juice to fill, and then add the remainder of the ingredients. Shake well and pour into a salt-rimmed pint glass.

2. Garnish with a celery stalk and your favorite pickled vegetables (or go as far as you want with it!).

A fully loaded Bloody Mary saves you a trip to the kitchen when hunger strikes, but the game is too good.

GLASSWARE: Pint glass
GARNISH: Pepperoni straw, celery stick, carrot spear,
buffalo wing, lime wedge

- 2 oz. vodka
- Tomato juice with Demitri's Chilies & Peppers Bloody Mary Seasoning, to taste

- Cold lager, to top

1. Build in glass with ice, starting with vodka and then fill to the top with tomato juice, leaving enough room to top with beer.

2. Garnish with pepperoni straw, celery stick, carrot spear, buffalo wing, and lime wedge.

• SMOKIN' MARY •

"I think it goes without saying that if you're smokin' ribs, the only garnish to have is a rib! Pulling brisket out of the smoker instead? Cut a tasty chunk and put it on the end of a bamboo skewer. Fire-roast a few veggie skewers and you're good! One of my favorite garnishes is a separate plate full of goodies instead of trying to balance a pound of stuff on top of the glass like a Flying Walenda." —Demitri Pallis

GLASSWARE: Pint glass or mason jar

GARNISH: See above.

- **2 oz. vodka**
- **Tomato juice with Demitri's Chipotle Habanero Bloody Mary Seasoning, to taste**

- **Orange juice**

1. Build in glass with ice, starting with vodka and then fill to the top using a 3:1 tomato-to-orange juice mixture.

2. Garnish as you deem fit.

HAND-BLOWN COCKTAIL GLASSWARE

TEGAN HAMILTON

Presentation is everything. Patrons drink not just with their mouth, but with their eyes as well, and nothing affects the attractiveness of a cocktail like the glass in which it is served. The right vessel will elevate a drink from ordinary to extraordinary, and that's where Tegan Hamilton comes in. The Australian native shaped her craft in Seattle's internationally-respected glass blowing community, earning fame for her signature pieces that feature octopus tentacles slinking their way up the sides of the glass. She was a contestant in Netflix's *Blown Away* series, and ships her pieces to buyers around the globe.

CREATIVE ICE

STEVE AND JUSTIN COX

"We started cocktail ice in Seattle," says Steve Cox, the founder of Creative Ice in Kent. Steve founded the company in 1985, creating ice sculptures for the Westin Hotel, a city landmark. Today, they are the only USDA-inspected cocktail ice company in Washington—one of the few in the nation, in fact—supplying dozens of Seattle bars and hotels with impeccable ice. "Cocktail ice is precision-based," explains Justin, Steve's son and co-operator of the company. "The water here in Kent is of such a high quality that we don't need to use reverse osmosis in our production." Rob Roy, the famed Belltown whiskey bar, was Creative Ice's first customer for cocktail ice in the city.

Steve told me that he was retired and that Justin was prepared to take over the operation, but when we met for the first time at their manufacturing plant, he was getting ready to cut a large ice sculpture for a local hotel.

"I thought you were done working?" I say.

He smiles. "I can't! We are just way too busy."

RACHEL'S GINGER BEER

RACHEL MARSHALL

Rachel's Ginger Beer was started by Rachel Marshall in 2010. She loved the bright, crisp ginger beer she had while living in Europe, and couldn't find a comparable product when she returned home to Seattle. She started making ginger beer late at night in the kitchen of a restaurant where she worked. She perfected the recipe and, with the help of her partner, Adam, began wholesaling to restaurants and bars as well as selling through the Capitol Hill farmers market. Within a couple of years, RGB had garnered such a devoted fan base that in 2013 Pike Place Market asked her to open her flagship store there.

• MOSCOW MULE •

A classic gets a spin with the crisp bite of quality ginger beer.

◆

GLASSWARE: Copper mug
GARNISH: Lime wheel and mint

- 2 oz. vodka
- 6 oz. Rachel's Ginger Beer

1. Add all of the ingredients to a copper mug with ice and stir.

2. Squeeze the lime over the drink and then place it on the mug rim and garnish the drink with mint.

• DARK AND STORMY •

Seattle knows dark days, but a drink like this makes those days brighter.

GLASSWARE: Collins glass

GARNISH: Lime wedge

- **6 oz. Rachel's Ginger Beer**
- **2 oz. Kraken Black Seal Rum**

1. Add the ginger beer to a collins glass filled with ice, stir, and top with the rum.

2. Squeeze the lime wedge over the drink and then drop it into the glass.

ABOUT THE AUTHOR

Neil Ratliff is the owner/operator of Emerald City Cocktails, the largest professional bartending service on the west coast. A native of Orlando, FL, he moved to Seattle in 2012 to complete his master's degree at the University of Washington and, after graduating, decided to remain in Seattle's thriving bar and cocktail scene and make the city his new home.

A two-decade veteran of the bar scene, Neil has been slinging drinks at bars and events in Orlando and Seattle since the law said he could. He earned his chops through TGI Fridays' exceptional bar training program, and after years of high-volume experience he joined the opening team of Vintage Ultra Lounge and Ceviche Tapas Bar in Downtown Orlando. To pay his way through graduate school, he crafted cocktails in Seattle's fine dining circuit until launching Emerald City Cocktails in 2016.

PHOTOGRAPHY CREDITS

Pages 4-5, 9, 21, 25, 27, 28-29, 36-37, 53, 76-77, 166-167, 174, 192, 198-199, 226, 232, 235, and 236 used under official license from Shutterstock.com.

Page 6 courtesy of the Library of Congress.

Page 30 Erika Schultz / The Seattle Times.

Pages 55-56, 59-60, 63-64, 67-68, 71-72, and 75 courtesy of Kathy Casey Food Studios and Angela Prosper.

Pages 133, 135-136, 139, 141-142, 203, 205-206, 209-210, 213, and 217 courtesy of Jason Anderson/OOLA.

Pages 158-160, and 162 courtesy of Jesse Stang.

Page 164 courtesy of Rachel Peterson.

Page 178 courtesy of Anne Watson.

Pages 219 and 221-222 courtesy of Jason Parker/Copperworks.

Page 229 courtesy of Demitri Pallis.

Pages 242 and 247 courtesy of Brooke Fitts/ Rachel's Ginger Beer.

Page 243 courtesy of Mercedes Hoerner / Rachel's Ginger Beer.

Page 244 courtesy of Jonathan Colton/Rachel's Ginger Beer.

All other photographs courtesy of Neil Ratliff/Emerald City Cocktails.

INDEX

–ABOUT CIDER MILL PRESS BOOK PUBLISHERS–

Good ideas ripen with time. From seed to harvest, Cider Mill Press brings fine reading, information, and entertainment together between the covers of its creatively crafted books. Our Cider Mill bears fruit twice a year, publishing a new crop of titles each spring and fall.

CIDER MILL
PRESS

BOOK
PUBLISHERS
KENNEBUNKPORT, MAINE

"Where Good Books Are Ready for Press"

Visit us on the web at
cidermillpress.com

or write to us at
PO Box 454
12 Spring St.
Kennebunkport, Maine 04046

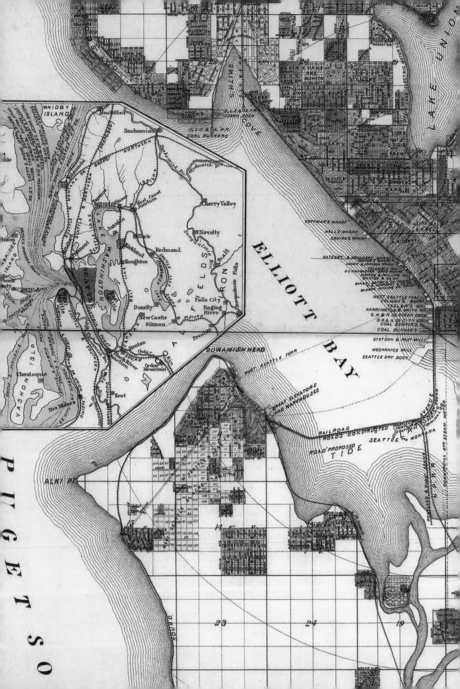